All the love,
Kathy

PAINFULLY HONEST

painfully honest

The Tale of a Recovering Helper

KATHY BROOKS

CONTENTS

V. How it Changed Me

I dedicate this, my first published book to the
beautiful country that is Ayiti.
O the things you have taught me.

Reviews For Painfully Honest

"I met Kathy down in Gonaives, Haiti, a not-so-frequent destination on this planet. What a pleasure to get to know her and her work with 2nd Story goods! She's an angel, hard at work, making this difficult world a little bit better. It's an honor to hear her story."

Rainn Wilson *Co-Founder LIDE Haiti, actor, comedian, podcaster, producer, and writer. Married to Author, Holiday Reinhorn, father to Walter. Perhaps best known as Dwight Schrute on The Office.*

"Kathy's words are vulnerable, sincere, and powerful. Through her own example and willingness to learn, Painfully Honest encourages everyone to ask hard questions and be open to learning new things. Her stories are encouraging, inspiring and will have you both laughing and crying."

Megan Boudreaux *Founder/Director Respire Haiti, Author, Miracle on Voodoo Mountain*

"In Kathy's first book, Painfully Honest: The Tales of a Recovering Helper, she writes vulnerably about her journey from the helper and little savior to partner, co-worker, and friend. These pages are packed with stories of loss and of love. She shares some of the beautiful things she learned and continues to learn. Kathy writes of failures and foibles and exposes her heart for the reader to both learn from and come to adore. Please read and enjoy this confessional book and allow it to help you become honest and introspective about yourself, I did."

Tara Livesay *Director & Midwife at Heartline Ministries - Haiti, Co-director at The Starting Place Birth and Wellness Center*

"An honest take on what struggling cultures really need from the Americans who come to help. This book is a must-read for anyone interested in entering other countries or cultures with a desire to serve and assist them. Find out what they really need and what you can really do for them."

Mandy Thompson *Artist, Journaling Coach, Creator of Analogue: A Field Guide for the Soul and founder of SoulSpace a Guide to Personalized Journaling.*

A raw page-turner. This book is a vulnerable reflection over a lifetime of good intentions. It is a no-holds-barred critical analysis of a self-professed do-gooder. It is delightful. It is exactly what the world needs right now. Kathy's voice is kind, routinely offering grace to herself and those around her, with honesty over the impact of their behavior. It is also a great, easy read!

Benjamin Brooks *Assistant Director of Policy, Whitman-Walker Institute*

This book is such a treasure and one that certainly lives out its title. Kathy leads with her heart and in this painfully honest narrative provides a transparent account of all her many steps and missteps as she tries to do good in another culture. Kathy's experiential wisdom is priceless! This book could serve as a practical orientation for anyone wanting to live and work in another culture. And, did I mention, I love the way she writes.

Dave Genzink *former Director Haiti Jobs Initiative, Partners Worldwide*

I truly think this book has something important for everyone. She speaks truths that apply to us all and communicates them in beautifully crafted short stories. Think Bob Goff meets Anne Lamott! Like me, you will laugh, cry, be humbled with her, and overall walk away with more wisdom. It reads easy and quick, but cuts deep and stays with you.

It will take you on a journey that shakes you to the core with pure truth, teaches you humility like you never thought you could know, and leaves you in utter awe at the kindness of God. I will keep reading it, over and over again, because I want to take it in and let it transform me. It's that kind of book. Someone get this book to Oprah or Brene!

Olivia Hosey *the intern in the book! 2018 Graduate Belmont University, Head of Marketing for 2nd Story Goods*

Sometimes, you just need
to hear that you're enough.

Which doesn't mean that
Sometimes you don't also
need to hear, Yeah,
you could be better.

Preface

Kai Skye says it well. "Sometimes, you just need to hear that you're enough. Which doesn't mean that sometimes you don't also need to hear. Yeah, you could be better."

For months I pushed the "writing a book" thing to the corner, the back burner, to the "I'll get to you one day" place. I have long wanted to write this book. It has been in me for years. The problem is that it seems frivolous.

To write.

There are so many immediate needs all around me. I can see from my porch, just steps away, people living off less than $3 a day. There are children too thin and houses too flimsy. I live in a land of job scarcity. And my job is to build a company that creates jobs.

Take time and write?

Frivolous.

But it's a new day. The young woman we brought on staff to help with 2nd Story Goods Marketing and Strategy came to Haiti and promptly let me know she had an agenda of her own.

Meet Olivia.

I met this young woman just before her freshman year of college. She was one of a dozen young ones who had come to Haiti on a two week trip with their Young Life Student Club to volunteer. As their leader went around the circle introducing me to each one, I thought to myself,

I will never remember their names, they all look alike to me.

And then she said, *This is Olivia.*

I shook her hand, said hello, and this Voice that often interrupts and overrides my brain said,

Pay attention to this one.

This one? I thought. Really? She looks just like the rest of them.

Just do it, the Voice said.

So bossy. I thought.

Later, the leader of the group took me aside and told me she felt like Olivia may very well be destined for life in Haiti after college. A real achiever, excelling at everything she puts her hand to. Not only that, her grandfather and father had worked in Haiti years earlier. There seemed to be a family calling.

That's interesting, I said, *it felt like Heaven marked her to me.*

And that was that. Never thought of that exchange again.

A year later, Renee asked if I had gotten an email from Olivia requesting to do an internship with us. Yes, I said. I think I did see that email. And, I ignored it.

This is going to sound terrible, I know. But the truth is that at that time, I felt I had no time for answering emails about interns. We were inundated with them. I am ashamed to admit that, interns were young people who had to be taken care of, taught how to live, shop for food, use public transportation and given something meaningful to do each day. You had to make sure they remembered to drink enough water so they didn't dehydrate and to wear sunscreen so they didn't die of sun poisoning. You had to watch them so they didn't go off with the first handsome boy that spoke a little English. They did weird things like "rescue" (read STEAL) baby goats from the community on the mountain because when they went hiking they found this newborn goat all by itself wandering the hill. Their hearts so good!
But then you have to explain that they just stole some family's tuition for their kids' school next year and now we have to hike back up there to return it. No one has time for that! I had carried over some residual bitterness. I admit. I had much to learn.

So, no. I didn't respond to the intern proposal.

But then she reminded me,

This is the girl you told me was "marked" to you. Like you are supposed to pay attention to her and respond to her when she emails you.

Oh.

That girl. Well.

She came that summer for 3 weeks. Our Big House in Gonaives was empty as most of the Americans had gone stateside to visit family, raise funds and take multiple trips to Chick-Fil-A.

Olivia came and we worked. And I quickly learned that she, like myself, was a Do-er. A deep thinker yes, but she accomplished things. Accomplishing things was and is my love language.

It also became apparent that we had similar thoughts on many social, spiritual and health-related issues, but we were not so much alike that she irritated me. In fact personality-wise, we were very different. She was peaceful and steady. I was wild and unpredictable. I could not handle another me. No one needed another me.

Fast forward three years. She graduated from college, moved to Haiti and began leading the newly formed Marketing Department of 2nd Story Goods.

But she also came with an agenda of her own.

To manage me. And get this book together.

The question was: Did I really want to write a book? Or just talk about it for another 10 years?

So under her management magic, I began to sneak away from the workshop at certain scheduled hours of the day, to be hidden and not get distracted, to not say to this book: *Everyone and everything is more important than you.* I began to wake at 4 am and quietly creep out to the dark kitchen table and open my bright screen and type.

I made an agreement with this young woman, Olivia, to finish writing and create this book.

So here it is. We got it done. Because even though I knew I was enough. I knew I was going to be loved and accepted whether I wrote this book or not. I also knew I could be better.

There is a lot in this book I could have left out. Perhaps I will wish very soon I did! Honest things, things still messy and unsolved. Things that break from the way it is commonly understood. Things I may learn I am wrong about. I have perhaps 20 more years on planet earth. That is not a lot of time. It is time to be unafraid to work these things out with a community of humans also on the journey.

There are scores of really important people not mentioned that are crucial to my story. The first draft was thick with names and sidebars about how I know each one. My wonderful editor trimmed it. You all know who you are.

I could write a book about each of you

Foreword

I was fascinated and curious from the first moment I encountered Kathy Brooks.

Now, don't misunderstand. Let the reader know, there are plenty of odd and interesting people to meet while working on the beautiful island of Haiti. But Kathy was more than odd and more than interesting.

Kathy was (and is) fascinating. I remember watching her from across a conference room in 2012 and thinking, *How old is that lady? She is spunky. She seems abstract, Hmmm, must be an artist;* I guessed correctly.

Over the next several years I got to know Kathy better as our husbands became close friends. We lived several hours apart but grabbed dinner or a night together when we could. We figured out bizarre things we had in common and traded woes and tips as the parents of many children. In the years of getting to know her, my initial take on Kathy was totally solidified.

This is a fascinating human.

If there were ever a time for humility and honesty in the arena of "missions" and "ministry", that time passed well over 200 years ago. However, as you may know, for decades and more the North American face of missions abroad has been somewhat stoic and proud, certain, colonizing, and condescending.

With all the answers and few (no?) questions asked of their host culture, Christian folks marched into foreign countries all over the world to fix them, save them, help them, change them.

Of course, we know now that much harm was caused. We learned that good intentions do not pave the glorious road to good outcomes and the stories to tell back at our home church are not necessarily the stories being told about us in our host lands. Our savior mentality and insensitivity to cultures unlike our own has been exposed.

In Kathy's first book, *Painfully Honest: The Tales of a Recovering Helper,* she writes vulnerably about her journey from helper and little savior to partner, co-worker, and friend.

These pages are packed with stories of loss and of love. She shares some of the beautiful things she learned and continues to learn. Kathy writes of failures and foibles and exposes her heart for the reader to both learn from and come to adore.

Kathy sums it up best when she writes:

Perhaps the greatest gift Haiti has given me as a recovering helper is the understanding that in reality there is no such thing as:

The helpers and the helped.

The haves and have nots.

The healers and the healed.

These are simply lazy ways to frame the world, so we can get on about our business.

Please read and enjoy this confessional book and allow it to help you become honest and introspective about yourself, I did.

Tara Livesay

I. In the Beginning

~ 1 ~

PERFECT MORAL CLARITY

"WHATEVER ELSE YOU MAY NEED TO GET CLARITY,
YOU MUST START WITH OPEN EYES."
SUSAN NEIMAN

My very first trip to Haiti:

We pulled over to the side of the road to pray. I saw her coming. A thin, somber-looking woman, perhaps in her mid-thirties, a baby cradled in her arms as she walked toward us. She approached the vehicle and waited patiently for us to look up. When we did my friend, Sherrie, in the driver's seat, spoke.

Sherrie is the friend who founded the school in Port Au Prince where we intended to volunteer. Small, red-headed and feisty, she loved the people in her community deeply.

The woman with the baby approached us with a softly spoken - *"Bonjou Madame."* And the conversation began.

For several minutes, while we sat still in the hot car, Sherrie and the woman chatted back and forth in a language I could not decode.

And then the woman turned, her baby still in her arms, and walked away.

What was that about? I asked.

Sherrie explained.

She came to ask us if we would take her child. She explained to me that she had 3 more children at home and she was struggling to find enough food for them daily. She desperately wanted to see her kids well fed and cared for. She was asking if we would take her baby and raise it or put it in our orphanage.

We didn't have an orphanage. But she didn't know that. She assumed we did.

I sat there in the back seat of Sherrie's old rusty Toyota 4Runner, sweat trickling down my neck, stunned. I had no grid for the event I had just witnessed.

And just then Sherrie turned around in her seat, looked straight back at me, and said the most important words.

You need to understand, she no more wants to give her child away than you do.

And that's when it happened. My moment of PMC: Perfect Moral Clarity.

I thought about my youngest child, our daughter Rebecca, who was four at the time. I tried to imagine what I would have to be feeling inside to be able to hand her over to a perfect stranger, not knowing if I'd ever see her again. What kind of desperation would drive me, or any mother to do such a thing.

As a young mother with my own precious babies, I know I would have fought to the death if a stranger tried to take any of them from me. And yet, I would indeed hand my daughter to a stranger, just like this woman, if I thought that was her only hope for survival. What mother wouldn't? What a tragic decision to have to make.

I thought for one minute about the woman's dilemma. And I asked myself, *What if she had another choice?* If I was in the same situation, what I would really appreciate is a job. Which would mean a way to make my life work, a way to keep my children.

And I knew at that moment I was being drawn to this beautiful warm, dusty place. I was drawn to somehow "help" though I had little idea what that word even meant or the mistakes I would make along the way.

~ 2 ~

LOST AT SEA

"OUR PRIME PURPOSE IN THIS LIFE IS TO HELP OTHERS,
AND IF YOU CAN'T HELP THEM, AT LEAST DON'T HURT THEM."
DALAI LAMA XIV

A few years ago a friend shared this analogy.

Once there was a woman and her children out at sea in a small fragile boat. A storm came up and their tiny vessel was tossed about and in danger of being lost in the waves.

Rescuers got word of the woman and others like her that were caught in this storm, struggling to keep themselves and their children alive. State-of-the-art rescue boats were equipped with fuel, food and warm blankets. Experts volunteered to join the operation to try to save them before it was too late.

Off they went flying over the sea to reach the woman and her children, desperate for help, in their precarious position. They reached the tiny boat, and for the first time, the woman exhaled in great relief, confident that they, at last, would be saved.

The volunteers reached with loving arms as the woman carefully handed over her children one by one to the kind helpers. Transferring them from her tiny unstable boat into their well-equipped ship.

Once the last one of her children was safely aboard, she turned to reach for their tattered bag of belongings. But when she turned back she saw that the rescue boat was circling away, headed to shore with her children looking back at her in disbelief.

The rescuers called out. "We'll take good care of them. God bless you! All the best! Make good choices!"

And I thought---
No. No. No.
This is not how we're going to do this.

~ 3 ~

BEFORE

Let me back up a few years.

When people ask me how we made the leap to move to Haiti. I tell them, it wasn't a leap, it was a thousand small steps. Twenty years before I met the woman asking us to take her baby, I married my forever person, Beaver Brooks. We became best friends and serious racquetball opponents while students at the University of Georgia. He started out as a lovable big brother to me and a handful of freshmen girls. But before long he and I were meeting for lunch without the others. Eventually, he put his arm around my shoulder as we walked through the historic parts of campus in Athens Georgia. He was becoming more.

We had the most traditional of wedding ceremonies, complete with puffy dresses and a church hall reception. We married just outside the Atlanta perimeter in Marietta, Georgia. We were babies at life and giggled our way through the sweetest of honeymoons, wearing ourselves out in the joy of knowing one another, in the most biblical sense! We came home and promptly moved to Texas,

22

where I would finish my degree at the University of Texas, while he pursued his Masters Of Divinity in Ft. Worth.

Three years later, in April of 1986, we moved to Vancouver Island where Beaver took a position as an Associate Pastor at a Baptist Church in the beautiful city of Victoria. This city is well known for its stunning flower baskets that hang from street lamps and spillover ornate concrete planters on nearly every street corner.

At that time Victoria was also somewhat known for its grand homeless population. Located off the west coast of Canada, Vancouver Island is affected by the North Pacific Ocean current that protects it from harsh conditions and brings warm weather it's way. The result is that the city of Victoria has the mildest winters in all of Canada. The temperature rarely dips below freezing.

When you are a person living outside in the elements, this is a big consideration. Add to that large open parks with long benches, parking garages with powerful heat ducts and generally nice people, and you can grow a fairly large homeless population with ease.

We loved the city! After some months living in an apartment, we found a tiny one-bedroom house with an above-ground basement and a darling picket fence. The city had marked it for demolition but it was still up for lease until they showed up with the wrecking ball. It was steps from a park and at the end of a dead-end street. We were young and in love and soon to have our first child.

The house was tiny, but we didn't need much space. And we knew we could outfit the basement and add a bedroom there. We also brought in a wood-burning stove to save on heating. We literally sawed through the living room floor upstairs to the tiny room downstairs that housed the woodstove. Then we strung up a box fan in the hole to blow the warm air up. Fancy.

Soon after getting settled into our house, we became distinctly aware of the homeless population and of the many young women soliciting for sex each night in the city center. Maybe this new awareness was because of our age or maybe it was a new perspective brought on by the fact that we had just become parents. Brandon James Brooks, our first child, was born in the summer of 1987 and with that, it felt like the whole world shifted.

Beaver would come home from work at the church at the end of the day and we'd sit together after dinner, dishes done, baby down, and we'd talk about the issue of homelessness. We both passed people daily who were sleeping on sidewalks and in alleys in our city. The truth is that he was always more content to "let things work themselves out," in connection to these social issues, while I was more intense and ready to leap into action. I think as a couple this was good tension. I was the passionate one, he was the steady, practical balance to that. And he was the one that carried through with the heavy lifting. But eventually, we both came to the same place in our minds. We were compelled to do something.

From the songs we sang in the church to the reading of the sacred texts we were bombarded with messages concerning our relationship with the poor and homeless and our willingness to help somehow. This, it seemed, was a foundational part of our faith.

Kinda.

At least we talked about it and sang about it. Many people volunteered in shelters and brought food to the food bank. I could do that part fine. But, I was too scared to actually do what felt like the next right thing: Bring homeless people into my actual house. Share our roof.

And this messed with me. I had the "all for you God" kind of conversion experience. Nothing halfway about it or about me. I was and remain smitten with this person known as Jesus. He was a rebel and an innovator. He wreaked havoc with the power brokers of his time and walked so kindly with the suffering ones. So my struggle to freely bring in the poor and homeless to my house was a thing. A big thing.

I was afraid that we'd meet a stranger on the street, and realize they were homeless. And it was going to be a particularly cold night, like that one night the temperatures did go below freezing. And I'd hear a voice say, "as you do it to the least of these you do it to me" and I'd stand there heart-stricken with the thought of leaving Jesus out in the cold. So we would invite this stranger to stay the night in our warm home and while we were sleeping they would get up and steal our stuff and leave. That was my basic fear.

So I started thinking about what stuff specifically I was afraid would be stolen. Our firstborn son, Brandon was still a newborn baby and he slept downstairs in the basement beside us, so there was no fear someone would steal him.

As I thought through our possessions I realized that we really didn't own anything of value. This was way before the day of computers and cell phones and small expensive speakers! We had nothing of value to steal. That is except, and this is where it gets embarrassing ... our China Cabinet.

We were gifted a lovely china cabinet from my mom when we moved to Canada. Then it dawned on me that was the single thing of value that we owned. When I shared this train of thought with Beaver? We looked at one another, like for real? And laughed. We laughed at the ridiculousness of my fear and ended up quite hysterical imagining anyone, especially someone without access to a moving van and a dolly, trying to steal our huge china cabinet!

O my.

Shortly after that, a lady wandered into our church service where we met in a local gymnasium. She seemed confused and her clothes communicated a lack of easy access to a washer and dryer. And we asked where she lived, she admitted that she had nowhere to stay.

Here it was, our Big Test.

And since we had settled the China Cabinet issue it was time to find out if we were all talk and no walk. Were we just blowing hot air with all our songs about God being a friend to the lost and giving shelter to the homeless? That was the question.

Not willing to fail this time, we invited her to come home with us. We already had a house full. By this time three beautiful kids of a friend were staying with us for a while, while mom took a break. And we had our baby son Brandon sleeping downstairs with us. I remember fixing the couch for her to sleep on and giving her some clothes to wear while we washed hers. We worked hard to figure out where her family was and see if we could find a way to get her there. I think she stayed a couple of days and then we managed to get her bus fare and headed back home.

There were many more folks after that. People on the margins of life. People like the old man we met after dinner one night downtown. We often took our leftovers out in to-go boxes knowing we'd probably, possibly, most likely find people that could use the calories just feet from the restaurant's door. This particular night we met an older man. He was frail and it was bitter cold. We offered to give him a warm bed to sleep in and he said ok. He climbed in our old VW van and was pretty quiet, answering our questions about his life and family with the smallest number of words. There was a battle going on inside of me the entire ride out of the city center. What if he is an ax murderer? What if he is not? What if he is sick or dying? What if he has a communicable disease and we're all going to get it?

And then ultimately I'd come to this one question:
What if this was my father?
How would I want people to treat him?

That question trumped the rest. Always. And that's how we ended up with a string of people sharing our home sometimes for months and sometimes only for hours, like this man who left in the night.

For years in Victoria, I was part of a small group of men and women that would "work" the streets for Jesus from 10 pm to 2 am, befriending the young women who walked the streets those hours, selling their bodies to the highest bidder. I can't really describe to you what these women went through night after night. It was the most foul and horrific of trades. Many nights I would stand with women talking about pregnancy, as I was almost always pregnant or nursing in those years, and many of them were too.

Yes. Truth. And still, they were forced out there in the winter months in stiletto heels and tiny pieces of clothing. So we'd be standing there talking as young women, and a certain car would come down the street and they'd warn me to back away.

Then I'd watch from the shadows as the men in cars would approach and make their picks of the flesh they wanted to buy. Some were rude and insulting, others hesitant as if ashamed. And I would want to scream at them "These girls are practically teenagers! These girls could be your daughters! Can you imagine what harm you are doing to them?" I wanted to rush the cars and scratch out these men's eyes and beat them with my fists. And at the same time, I knew that the men that owned these young women were watching. They were invisible but always watching their investment. The only reason the girls were allowed to talk to us is that we seemed harmless and we bought the girls hot chocolate and gave them gifts when we learned they were expecting or had a birthday.

I do know that there are men and women that identify as self-employed sex workers and see this as a legitimate trade. They lobby to have this legalized so that they can get equal protection under the law. But I want to make clear that this is not what I witnessed on this block of downtown Victoria, BC. These young women were controlled by others. They were being used and abused. They were being trafficked.

I remember one young girl. I'm going to call her Anne. She was fresh into the business. She broke my heart a thousand times over as I begged her each week to come home with me. Her pimp was mean and watched her like a hawk. She was addicted to the drugs he gave but she was also terrified of him. One night I walked up and down the street looking for her. When I finally found her I could see the dark bruises under her thickly applied makeup. As calmly as possible I begged her to come with me. To let me help her escape. She seemed the tiniest bit open, so I walked to the corner phone booth and phoned Beaver and had him head our way in the van, just in case she possibly agreed.

With Anne, I talked softly yet with as much urgency as I could like you would a wounded kitten you were trying to woo out from under a porch so you could bandage its broken leg. Eventually, she said yes. But we had to go first to her room to get her belongings.

We walked calmly down the block, so as not to draw attention. We rounded the corner and entered the dark lobby of a sleazy hotel and that's when I realized we were going to the room where she "worked".

I wanted to throw up and pass out and scream all at the same time. But there was no time for that. We knew if he, the guy that claimed ownership to her, came back and saw us it would not go well. We ran up the shadowed stairs and found the door where her key turned the knob. She busted into the room and grabbed a black duffel bag and began stuffing in the belongings she called her own. I remember looking around the dirty room-- the smell, the unmade bed, the drugs laying in the open--and wanting to get her as far from that place as possible. Everything about it reeked of darkness and death.

Shaking, we raced down the stairs and out the door just as Beaver came driving down the street. I remember he pulled over and I gave Anne the front seat and I climbed in the back. We laughed at how that scene might have looked to the casual passerby. This sounds hard to believe now, even as I write it so many years later, but this is the life we led. For me, all I could ever think was, what if this were my daughter? How would I want people to treat her?

I'd love to end this story of Anne with the narrative I dreamed up for her. I'd love to say she stayed with us for a few months, got into a rehab facility, was reunited with her family, started a great job that she loved, found the man of her dreams, had kids, and lived happily ever after. That was my dream for her. This is how I would have saved her. Me rushing in, the hero, pulling her out of that awful situation with the strength of my love and helper's heart.

But the truth is I don't know what happened to Anne. Sometime in the wee hours of the morning, she left our house. Before we woke up to make her a big welcome breakfast. Before our little boys could give her hugs and ask her to read them a book. Before we could sit and listen as she poured out her pain. She left.

I never saw her again.

Over the years I have collected many renditions of this story. Girls that got so so close. I can probably point to one or two that I know made it out alive. Not because of anything I did but because of the decisions they were ready to make for themselves. Ultimately that is what matters. Every addict will tell you that.

Anne likely doesn't remember me, but I will always remember her. She was a part of the journey that led me to the next. So, when people ask me how we made the leap to move to Haiti. I tell them, it wasn't a leap, it was a thousand small steps.

~ 4 ~

A FAMILY OF ARTISTS

"HOPE, EVEN MORE THAN NECESSITY,
IS THE MOTHER OF INVENTION."
JONATHAN SACKS

I brought paints and brushes with me on that first trip to Haiti when I met the woman asking us to take her baby.

The trip came about because Beaver and second son, Taylor had participated in a week-long mission trip 6 months earlier with a group of volunteers from a local church. Taylor was 13 at the time and was deeply impacted by those 7 days in rural Haiti. He came home, dismantled his bed, and slept on the floor for almost 2 years to show solidarity with teenagers who slept on floors. Watching him intrigued me. I had to go.

So there I was on my first trip, paint supplies in hand. No real idea what to do with them. My grandmother was the well-known artist, Reba Sweat, and as a little girl, I would sit for hours and watch her paint. When I was older she let me set up a canvas right beside her in her studio. That space was magic to me, smelling of turpentine and surrounded by clipped pictures of exotic faces and colorful

landscapes. Thick pads of giant paper held charcoal sketches, each
one a masterpiece in the works. At some point, I became keenly
aware that her work was featured in local galleries and people paid
real dollars to own one of her originals. It was then I realized that
art could also be business.

Once I began to have children of my own I began stretching my
wings with the creative. In Victoria, BC I would sit with my young
sons, brushes in hand, and we'd paint on long rolls of paper creating one continuous work of art. Then, inspired by whimsical pieces I
saw in the shops downtown, I began painting furniture: chairs with
graphic flowers and tables with favorite quotes.

Brandon, Taylor, Cory Ben, and Sam were born during our ten
years in Canada. Yes, I gave birth to four strapping baby boys in
barely six years.

And in 1996 we returned to our roots in Georgia to raise them.

The truth is that my body was worn out. Between pregnancies,
nursing infants, and being deeply involved in the lives of our com-
plex community, I was running on empty by the time we landed
back home in the South.

We settled on St. Simons Island, in an old windswept beach
house loaned to us, rent-free for a few months by a very generous
couple. We were able to use this place of peace to take a much-
needed deep breath. My soul, like my body, had been worn thin.

I was in need of full restoration, beside still water. In this season
I began to realize I had embraced a Savior Mentality that had me
thinking my value came from my capacity to *change the world*. The
need to stay in Helper mode had worn me down. A strong young
woman with four young kids, I found it hard to take breaks and rest

when there were still people in need. The move to Georgia was good for me. The house on the beach might have saved my life.

Beaver found a job with a local property rental company doing repairs and upkeep on their units. And I concentrated on raising sons and teaching them the ways of the South. Important things like, Yes Ma'am and No Sir and how to sort out the English language spoken in "Southern".

By 2000 we had found our dream property and moved out to the country. It was a five-acre piece of land on a four-lane US highway about 25 miles from the closest Walmart. That tells you how far out in the country it was!

We moved because we wanted our kids to know that water comes from wells driven deep in the earth and to know how to both identify trees and climb them. I wanted the freedom of land: space for the boys to make as much noise as they wanted without fear of bothering neighbors. I dreamt of this space to plant gardens and have chickens and a few goats. I had never lived in the country as a kid. But I had read stories and had seen movies about it. I tended to think that made me an expert on things.

We renovated the old four-bedroom house and bought mud boots for everyone. By this time we had our beautiful baby girl, Rebecca Addie. Though a surprise, she was wanted and loved from the instant we learned of her existence. As a mother of many sons, people often asked me if we were going to keep trying to get a baby girl. Honestly, I had let go of that idea between boy number two, Taylor Russell, and boy number three, Cory Benjamin. And when Samuel Frazier, number four in the line up came out a boy, I was truly thrilled. I was the mother of four boys. It fit.

But when I was pregnant with Rebecca and went to have the first sonogram and the technician told us we were having a baby girl, a hidden door sprang open that unleashed joy from a deep deep place in my soul. Tears streamed down my face and into my ears as I lay on that table, goop spread across my belly. A girl. Like me. A girl!

Rebecca Addie was born near the end of 1998. She came home to four adoring big brothers. She grew up on the farm with them carrying her on their backs through the woods, playing soccer in the big field beside the house, pretending she was scoring goals and a real team player. They spent summers teaching her to swim and letting her have the best floats in the spring-fed pond that was the center of our land. Like my own childhood--running up and down the creek and playing football in the field near our home--we made this our dream space with gardens and tree forts, a greenhouse and an art studio in the shed. It was our own little paradise.

Enter Art and Business.

At some point, Brandon and Taylor began building wood benches from scrap lumber and asking me to paint them. Sam got on a kick making these 4-foot wooden crosses that I turned into mosaic folk art. I still have an old window that Rebecca painted as a three-year-old! We then loaded up the family van with our precious works of art to peddle to high-end boutiques on St. Simons Island where local people who owned lovely beach houses and tourists from Atlanta came to shop. They were a hit. Or I should say the kids were a hit and generous shop owners bought everything we had and asked for more. Such is the beginning of what became Sunny Brooks Farm. The family business.

I was a mom, and with the materials at hand, we were making art and making business. And though Beaver had a job at the time, as is the case with many families, some months lasted longer than the paychecks did. So with the humble profit of our art business, we were buying groceries and tennis shoes and school supplies. It was the model I inherited from my grandmother and instinctively created for myself and our family.

It was what I knew, and certainly the reason I landed with paint and brushes in my suitcase on that first trip to Haiti.

~ 5 ~

PAINTED ROCKS

"IT'S BEAUTIFUL TO ME"

KATHY BROOKS

Paints and brushes in hand. I took stock of what resources were available around the city of Port Au Prince and all I saw were rocks. I knew I could make art out of just about anything. I was used to the generous dumpsters in Georgia sitting at worksites where piles of unwanted wood were thrown daily. But here, there was no wood. No tin. No old chairs or windows to paint on. Everything is recycled many times over. Nothing is left on the side of the road. There are no big dumpsters at work sites. Here in Haiti, every shred of building material is wanted. It is all used. There is no waste.

But there were rocks! The best kind of rocks. Big smooth rocks. Everywhere. All over the sides of the roads. For Free!

So we put out a word in the surrounding community that we were looking for people that wanted to try out for work as artists. We would accept anyone that could paint. We gathered a few rocks and carted them to the small nearby church, led by a dearest and wise Haitian couple, where we were able to set up shop for a few days.

Over 100 people crowded in that small space on that first day. We told them at the end of three days we would determine the artists among us and start a rock painting group.

That was the extent of my business plan.

Men and women and teenagers and kids turned out for the trial. We carefully poured paint onto paper plates. We handed out cheap brushes and cans of water for rinsing. And Rocks. It didn't take long until our supply was done and people just started going out into the street and finding their own. They were there in abundance.

We watched as they painted. Some went right to it as if they thought that if they painted fastest they would get chosen. Some took their time being painstakingly careful to paint precious detailed flower petals and perfectly shaped mangoes.

As it were, some were talented. Some, not at all. But there was no shortage of hope in that room. By day two I was getting to know people's personalities a bit, names even, and I was beginning to feel the pressure of the decisions I had to make the next day. Stressful. I wanted to pick them all. I wanted to give work to all.

This was my baptism into the water I swim in to this day.

Day Three arrived and we carefully went over all the rocks, pulling out the best ones. Everyone had been instructed to paint their names on the bottom of the rocks. So after much prayer and stress, we chose our group of 6 painters and called their names. What a catch 22! For each person chosen, there were 15 not chosen! There was agony and ecstasy in that room. Hope crushed and hope revived.

We stayed late and paid everyone something for the best of the rocks that we would take back to Georgia. And informally we decided to gather with our newly formed group again when I returned in a few months.

It was dark and raining by the time we were packed up and were ready to go back to Sherrie's guest house school. We had all our precious rocks loaded up in the wheelbarrow someone had loaned us. My son, Brandon, who had traveled down with me, strained his back hauling that heavy wheelbarrow through the streets and down the tiny allies. One section along the way was so narrow that you could only go through it one person at a time.

This rainy night as we rounded the corner of that particularly narrow part of the path, there we were, 7 oblivious Americans walking single file, caught off guard by a man, naked, covered in soap, all lathered up, taking a shower in the downpour. Why not? It was dark out. It would have been a relatively private place if it weren't for the optimistic white ladies and the huge white teenager pushing a wheelbarrow of freshly painted rocks down the path. Awkward does not begin to describe how we passed by him and all his bubbles in that space.

So this was how we began.

Painting rocks.

At one point in that week, I remember stepping away and climbing the ladder to the upper floor of the church that was under construction. As people were painting rocks below I began to seriously second guess myself.

What am I thinking? This is insane and ridiculous and I have no idea what to do next.

And I heard a Kind Voice in my head say, Well, it's beautiful to me.
And I thought, ok then.
That's enough.

In my journal I wrote:
life is pretty simple.
love. share. paint. weep. hug.
get a shower when you can.
holy holy everywhere.
Haiti.

We boarded our American Airlines flight with rocks in our suitcases. Proudly. We got strange looks from the US Customs agent when he inspected our bags. I was so darn proud of those rocks! Some were quite lovely: birds, houses, pineapples. The stories of the ones who painted them tumbled from my mouth and Mr. Customs Man just stood and stared.

We arrived back in Georgia to this now foreign planet called the U S of A. I'll never forget the strange sensation of coming back after only 7 days away, into the atmosphere of what now felt like a distant galaxy. This land filled with electricity and homes with running water and smooth roads AND stores with SO MUCH STUFF had become foreign. It was completely overwhelming.

My first trip to Walmart after coming back was a disaster. I yanked free a buggy and walked bravely in, prepared to shop for a family of seven as was my custom. But as I started through the store I could feel my heart crumbling beneath the weight of each overflowing aisle of cereal choices and diaper brands. I looked at myself and other shoppers. We weren't the elite, the ultra-wealthy. I dare say we may have even been considered from the lower rung of the economic ladder, yet still, we had all of this merchandise within reach, easily available to us and our families.

So why not them? Why not the Haitian families that lived in the very margins of existence? Surely we had done nothing to deserve such abundance. Nothing. Surely the Haitian mothers and fathers worked equally if not many times over as hard as we did. My brain couldn't process it. I had just come from a neighborhood where newborns were placed on the cleanest piece of cardboard their big brother could find. That was his welcome home. And here on these shelves were little machines that warm the disposable wipes we used to clean our babies' bums.

I cracked.

The tears held back as long as possible but then one got through and there was no stopping. My apologies for whoever had to handle that cart half-filled left in the middle of aisle 6 that day. I heaved myself out the automatic opening doors through the parking lot and to the private sanctuary of my family van to weep and rage against the injustice of it all.

I was angry. Sad. But mostly, angry.

SIDEBAR: And this is by far the most common reaction we find when people leave Haiti on their first visit and return home. Anger.

The problem is we really don't know who we should be angry with or what constructive thing we should do with that anger.

Now, years later, we know to counsel teenagers that come to Haiti to visit. On their last day, we let them talk about how they feel about going back to their lives in America. They have so much to process. We tell them clearly that they are likely to go home and feel a lot of anger. It is important for them to know that it is not the fault of their parents that the kids they met in Haiti don't have what they have. The fact that they have many pairs of shoes does not keep these kids in some neighborhoods in Haiti from having shoes. This is not a zero-sum game. There are more than enough resources in the world. WAY more than enough.

Economics is how they shift.

Purchasing products made from people in these spaces is a way to make a difference. Investing in education and small businesses makes lasting change. We tell them to please instead of just being angry, channel that energy into some good action.

END of SideBar.

Rocks.
We added the painted rocks from Haiti to the product line of our expanding family "cottage industry" of hand-painted signs, mosaic crosses, mirrors and benches. Then we charged our way into the Atlanta Gift Mart. And by charged I mean we used our credit card to pay for the entire thing. This was the only way I knew to find people to buy them, at first. So we paid for a 10 x 10 booth in the Artisan area of the world's largest retail trade show. We put it all on our credit card: booth, food, travel expenses... nearly 10k by the time it was all done.

The show began and buyers came into the booth attracted by the hand-painted pithy quotes on our colorful signs and the unique mirrors and painted benches. We'd steer them over to our unique selection of hand-painted rocks that we had literally just brought home from Haiti a week ago! We'd dazzle them with the stories of the amazing women who painted the rocks and the good that this start-up business would do. I think we sold a whole three.

It was a failure.

We did get orders for signs, benches, and mirrors. But not enough to pay for the adventure of being there. It took us years to pay off that credit card debt.

So we did what any reasonable business person would do. We quit? No. We did it again six months later.

But this time I went back to Port Au Prince with trending designs, specific colors, quotes and words to go on the rocks. We gathered our small group of painters and sat for days in the shade of my friend Sherrie's generous porch and together we painted rocks while they tried to teach me bits of their mother tongue, Kreyol.

As I sat with them and heard their stories, I began to fall under the spell. Haiti is a very dangerous place. Most everyone that comes here falls under the spell of the beauty and strength and fierce courage of her people. The infectious joy seeps from her heart into your own. Please be careful and guard yourself if you think of visiting.

We painted enough rocks to have a healthy stock. And we carted the suitcases of stones back to America, again.

We pulled out the old credit card and went back to the Atlanta Gift Mart. Except for this time we bought artsy brown craft boxes with colorful shredded paper to nest the rocks. We had a color scheme and trending words and quotes by Erma Bombeck. We were armed for success. We hauled our old doors and shutters and built our rustic 10 x 10 ft. booth. We printed the catalog I made myself and off we went!

What I'd like to report here is that the new designer rocks were a big hit and that we sold them all and got reorders for hundreds more. But we did not. We did sell more than 3. But no one would call this a success. A valiant effort, but not a success.

~ 6 ~

SUNNY BROOKS MARKETPLACE

"AND THOSE WHO WERE SEEN DANCING WERE THOUGHT TO BE IN-
SANE BY THOSE WHO COULD NOT HEAR THE MUSIC."
FRIEDRICH NIETZSCHE.

The era of the painted rocks died down but our love for Haiti did not.

Haiti became a part of our lives. Three to four times a year someone from our family was there, Beaver, me, or one of our teenage sons. Miraculously, Sherrie Fausey from the school in Port Au Prince would faithfully meet us at the airport, her distinct red hair and pale arms, standing out in the crowd as she waved to us from the sidewalk. How very glad we were that she continued to welcome us into her home and school all those years! We would sit with students learning to read in their third language, English, amazed at their young brilliance. We'd do science experiments with fourth graders and talk World History with the older ones. Each trip we came to teach, but each time we were the ones that learned.

This is also where we met our now son, Kervens Louis.

When he was five years old, his birth family experienced a tragic loss where they lived in a nearby neighborhood. That led his mom to make the difficult decision to move from the region. She came to Sherrie Fausey and asked if there was a safe place for Kervens to live so that he could stay in her school. It was essential to her that he stay in this school where he was flourishing.

I can only imagine the agony she went through. Like so many mothers around the world, she sacrificed her own heart to give her child the best chance at health and the bright future she could imagine for him.

Sherrie agreed to find a good home for him and soon he moved into the home of Sherrie's good friend Dorothy Pearce. Dorothy was a semi-retired legal secretary when she came to Haiti on what was supposed to be a week-long mission trip, and stayed. She returned to the states weeks later to resign her position at the law firm and prepare to move to Haiti full time. She had discovered her passion for children needing intensive medical care.

It was too easy for those kids and their parents to fall between the cracks of the healthcare system. She also realized that many came from far-reaching zones out in the country and that they needed a stable place to live while they went through treatments in the capital city, Port Au Prince. This drew her to rent a house in the same area as Sherrie's school. Here she gave short-term respite care and found medical help for children that were sick and others with special needs. Parents stayed involved in the well-being of their children and many of the kids were able to go back home once they were stable. She loved big. She loved well.

Around this same time, we had saved up the money to go to Haiti with our entire tribe for two months in the summer. Beaver was able to work remotely at his new sales job as long as he had internet and phone access. Our boys ranged in age from 12 to 17 and Rebecca was 5. School was out and Sherrie was headed stateside for fundraising, but still needed someone in the house to keep projects going and the summer feeding programs stocked up with supplies.

It was in this setting that we got to know Kervens Louis, now referred to as Kevs. He was bright and picked up the English language quickly. Even as a child he was translating for the eager medical teams that came to offer free clinics in Haiti. He had to grow up fast as each month, he was pulled into serious grown-up conversations. The kid learned more about the female reproductive organs and cancerous growths than any child really should!

Kevs and Rebecca are basically the same age, and they were inseparable from the time they woke until the time they passed out exhausted from heat and soccer at the end of the day. To Brandon, Taylor, Ben, and Sam, he became a little brother.

They gently tossed him around as they wrestled, a sure sign of family inclusion, and read books with him at night. That summer we became a family. Dorothy was the in-house grandma that made up the silly songs we sang together around the dinner table. She was the one that bonded us, comforted us, and brought wisdom in the difficult days. Beaver and I were the parents and the 6 kids were just that. We cooked, ate, laughed, prayed, and worked together. We were one big family. And I found my heart bonded to this kid, Kevs.

Leaving to go back to the states at the end of those two months shredded me. I remember asking God,

What do you know that I don't know? How do you believe that I can actually survive leaving him? Do you really think my heart will continue to beat once I get on that airplane? And what of his mother? Where is she? Is she well? Will she return for him?

So little I knew then of what was to come. So little I knew of what my heart would yet be asked to endure!

We returned to Georgia pretty certain we were going to hear from Heaven that it was time to sell everything we owned and move our giant family to Haiti for good. Our loose plan was that we would find a small house to rent, perhaps near our friends in Port Au Prince and begin to help them with the many projects that needed to get done and try to establish some means of economic development.

We'd use the money from the sale of our farm and all our things to finance it. Surely we could raise "missionary" support from a church in the area to help? That was a loose idea. We just knew we wanted to go back with our children and use what we had to relieve what we saw as crushing poverty and the lack of jobs.

But here is the problem.

It was mine and Beaver's daily spiritual practice to sit with God.

Whatever that means to you, this "sitting with God" for us meant reading a bit from the sacred text and then talking and listening. This is where things started to go south.

The listening part.

Unbeknownst to him, I was getting the strong message from this sitting time. "Not now. Haiti is in your future, but not now." And for me, heaven seemed to need to add the emphasis, "Don't pretend that you don't hear me. If you get this wrong and don't listen, the consequences are going to affect more people than yourself."

Dang.

Fortunately (or unfortunately) Beaver was getting the same message. His was a bit more cryptic. "I want you to do here what you will do in Haiti."

Ok. No idea what that means, but ok.

But that "not now" made me angry.

I said to Heaven, *Fine. If you won't let us move to Haiti, then we are going to get serious about working in this community. We'll show you!* I said, shaking my fist to the sky. God, surely so very frightened!

Since moving to the farm, we'd become involved in a loving, small, local church. We were leading the youth group. Far too many of the kids had stories of parents that were in prison or rehab facilities. We loved it when kids came in to share the exciting news that mom or dad were coming home. It was not uncommon for this scenario to take place. We were a small south Georgia town equally filled with unscathed families and families being ravaged by the narcotic production industry: primarily people cooking meth for distribution. What many of the kids in our area had already witnessed and lived through was unspeakable. Eventually, the mom or dad would end up in prison or rehab. And when these kids got word that their parents were coming home, they had so much hope. At least the young ones did.

The rehabilitated parents were celebrated when they walked back through the doors of the church Sunday morning. We were encouraged when they returned the next week and joined a Sunday school class. But too often, fueled by constant temptation and the lack of available jobs for people with a prison record, many fell back into the life-threatening, family-crushing trade of meth-making.

In our rebellion toward this mean God that would not let us move to Haiti, we said, Fine. We're going to do something about THIS.

Having already learned the sacred art of work we went W A Y out on a limb. So instead of selling the farm and moving to Haiti, we refinanced our farm and used the funds to lease a vacant building a mile down the highway, and began renovations.

Our vision was to create a space that holds the environment of heaven and runs like a business so people could be employed there and get themselves healed and whole... with or without a prison record. We had spent a few years working with the youth. Now it was time to get serious about the parents.

And so the Sunny Brooks Marketplace was created as a means of economic and cultural change in our small South Georgia town.

This rambling 10,000 square foot building became home to a coffee shop, restaurant, pottery studio, business center with internet and shipping facilities, garden center and secondhand store! It was a thriving hub of activities.

We were warmly embraced by the local AA, NA, and Al-Anon groups. We held weekly parenting classes for parents working to regain custody of their children. We had big Spaghetti Dinners for the

Community to come out and Meet the Candidates when it was time for local elections.

A friendly group of retired and on-the-way-to-work men would gather at the back round table for morning coffee, toast, eggs, and bacon. They'd sit with the local newspaper and solve all the world's problems while we kept their mugs filled with steaming hot coffee.

Either Beaver or I, usually both of us, would be there to open up. He was the better cook, I was the better server. We eventually attracted experienced servers and chefs who knew their way around a kitchen and served up remarkable, fresh healthy meals.

Friday and Saturday nights we also served dinner. We started early, filling tiny vases with fresh-cut flowers and lighting votive candles so that each table was an invitation to something special. Whenever possible we added live music those nights. Local bands signed up to play. We had a famous Blues musician that always drew a crowd. And other bands that did covers of the best of 80s rock, sprinkled with some original pieces and a dash of contemporary Christian. Often on those nights, Beaver and I would make our way to the dance floor and he would swing me around when they played our song, "Brown Eyed Girl".

Those nights were hectic and yet sweet. We were a mix of volunteers from local churches and precious folks recovering from abuse or who had just gotten home from rehab. Some were carpenters by day and grill masters by night. We loved one another. We were there for each other. And we loved the community.

We saw people change the trajectory of their own lives as a result of time in this space. At one point I painted hopscotch on the concrete pad leading up to the front door. People would walk in and say, what is this place? It feels like a cross between church and the hippie hostel down the road!

For us, it was our training ground.

~ 7 ~

2010 THE EARTHQUAKE IN HAITI

"YOU CAN MEASURE THE EARTHQUAKE BUT YOU
CANNOT MEASURE THE HEARTBREAK."
DR.P.S. JAGADEESH KUMAR

I remember exactly where I was. I was supposed to have already left work, but I was running late. I was standing in the office of Sunny Brooks Marketplace when the phone rang and a man I didn't know said he had just talked to our friend Dorothy in Haiti and that she and Natasha were alive.

Alive? What?

Natasha Jovin is a young woman I had met in Haiti years earlier. Girl was on fire with justice and truth-telling. I fell in love with her and eventually, she came to be a part of our family, home, and work in Georgia. At the time of the earthquake, she was in Haiti helping

Dorothy with the medical care of the kids in her home. She was like a daughter to me.

When I answered the phone I didn't know yet about the quake. This phone call came in only moments after the earth had stopped shaking. All the man said was that Dorothy and Natasha were alive and that they didn't have any information about the kids at her home because they were on the road to the hospital on the other side of Port Au Prince when it happened.

Natasha had screamed our phone number into the phone as Dorothy used the last minutes of the working cell tower to let her brother, this stranger to me, now on the phone, know she was alive. He said he lost the connection after that and he could not get her back. Till the day I die, I will be thankful to Natasha for having the strength of mind to give him our number.

As he was still talking everything went into slow motion. All I could think about was Kevs, the son we were adopting. Several years had passed with no communication from Kevs' birth mother and no one was able to find her or reach her by phone. Legally he was eligible for adoption while living with Dorothy. Though there were mountains of paperwork yet to be processed, we already felt like he was part of our family. Was he hurt? Was he alive? Who was with him and the other kids? I lunged toward the computer on the desk. Emails started coming in and while still on the phone I began seeing the news.

Haiti earthquake. Catastrophic magnitude. 7.6. Buildings down. Unknown numbers dead.

I searched the emails quickly but they were all asking us for information, not giving it. I remember calling Brandon, our oldest son. He was living in California with his beautiful wife Whitney. Being the oldest in the tribe of kids, he is the one we call first with the news that needs to be dispersed to the rest. He has to do those hard things. Oh, the weight the oldest child does carry! Surely I was in shock as I told him about the earthquake. The news was just hitting stations there as well.

I was a little mad. Like crazy mad not angry mad. It was not knowing if Kevs was alive or if a falling building had killed him or left him injured or if he was unsafe because of chaos in the streets. I was terrified with the thousand what-ifs.

I remember Brandon and Whitney calling back a little later from California and saying to me, "Mom, we've got Kevs. We're going to hold him in prayer for you all night from California to Haiti. We'll surround him and protect him. We have him for you mom."

Dang. I'll never forget that conversation. What a son and daughter-in-law. They knew.

My first reaction was to get a plane ticket. I scrambled onto the American Airline website to secure a seat on the next flight to Port Au Prince. That was within the hour after the earthquake had hit and commercial airlines still thought they could land. I bought a seat on the next available flight but within hours that fell apart. All commercial flights were canceled.

Sometime later we found out that Kevs had been playing soccer at the nearby church field when it struck. He was shaken and confused and made his way back home to Dorothy's. He was the oldest kid by far and when he arrived he found the nannies and kids scared and making their way into the yard to create safe spaces and makeshift beds. It happened late in the afternoon and by then it was beginning to get dark. Everyone slept outside that night. Most people slept out from under concrete roofs for many weeks and months that followed.

In Port Au Prince, the capital city of Haiti with over 2 million people, many, many buildings collapsed. People later called it not a natural disaster, but an engineering one. In many buildings that didn't fall, walls were cracked and ceilings buckled. It was like a terrifying war zone that shook again and again as aftershocks made their way through the earth. Dust covered the entire region as people climbed out of the collapsed buildings bloody and broken. Others never did.

Beaver was able to get on a flight with MFI, a mission aviation company, within about 48 hours. Our big concern was Sherrie Fausey, (our dear friend and the principal of the school where we often stayed and worked). There was a lack of communication and no one had heard from her. Beaver's priority was finding her or her body. A doctor friend brought Beaver a body bag for him to pack in his luggage. "Just in case," he said.

Beaver arrived in Port Au Prince on one of the first flights in. He found a moto-taxi to take him to the school. And there he found Sherrie shaken, bruised, and scraped up, but very much alive! He spent the next 7 days as part of a sea of walking wounded and international helpers working together to create pieces of order out of the chaos. Her beautiful home that was also the school was gone. She barely escaped with her life. A young boy, the precious son of a family who had an apartment on the site, did not. The sorrow over losing this child crushed us all.

Beaver and Sherrie worked with other staff and helpers to set up camp in the construction site of the new building that was already underway and created a base camp for her and the kids. So many kids.

There are books written about the days following this tragic event. Probably many more should be written by the survivors and helpers that showed up. Those are not my stories to tell. I could never do them justice.

I arrived 6 days later with a small group of people carefully chosen by me. By this time I had come and gone to Haiti many times. Sometimes alone and sometimes with a group of volunteers who wanted to experience Haiti and somehow help. Pretty much anyone that volunteered was accepted on those trips. But this time I was extremely picky about who I would take with me. Beaver was relaying information to me about what skills were most needed at the moment.

So I chose Taylor Brooks, our second-born son and the one who, of all our kids, had spent the most time in Haiti as a teenager. He was just turning 21 that week. Taylor had always been the one to call when a building needed building or a broken thing needed fixing. He was obvious. Plus, he was a son.

Kelly Morgan was my next pick. Kelly was a young nurse I had known since she was a kid. She was smart, really good at her job, full of faith, and easy to work with. She was a joy. After that, I chose JT Kowalachuck, a young man with a brilliant engineering mind. He was all about logistics and ended up being incredibly valuable for meeting with top people from the UN and designing systems to safely distribute food and water.

Next, I chose Adam Pelletier. The best way to describe Adam is to say he is part Boy Scout, part Special Ops, and part really good dad. He is about the most strong, kind-hearted man you'll ever meet. Not so macho that he has to slay dragons (but he will gladly if he needs to) but the kind that knows how to get water to come out of the pipe. He and Taylor together were a dream team.

The last member of the group was a woman who was a stranger to me then. Martha Hanna. I had received a phone call from her a couple of days before we were to fly. She heard we were going and she was volunteering to go with us. Now, years later, she reminds me how borderline rude I was on the phone. I didn't really want to hear her conversion story or how she loved children and felt led to help Haiti. I needed to know what kind of experience she had working as a nurse in the developing world and that she could pee in a bucket if need be!

I told her I'd get back to her. I remember really wavering about this decision. In the past I watched people come to Haiti and unknowingly end up becoming the focus of the group's energy because of their incapacity to deal with the precarious situations we found ourselves in. There was a thin line between helping and hurting. And I knew this trip wasn't the time to risk it.

Eventually, I sensed the thumbs up for this mystery woman and told her to meet us in Ft. Pierce, Florida the next night. We'd be at the Days Inn to sleep and then we'd get to the airstrip the next morning to wait in line to get a seat on a flight.

The next day we drove all afternoon and arrived late in Ft. Pierce, had a quick meal, and went to bed. Martha hadn't arrived so I left a key to the room Kelly and I were sharing at the front desk for her.

I'll never forget waking up the next morning looking at the person waking up just 24 inches away from me and saying, "You must be Martha."

We were instant friends.

We landed in Port Au Prince and went through the makeshift customs hanger that was handling the people and supplies coming into the country. I don't even know how things were that organized in those early days. I saw my husband for the first time in 8 days and man did he stink! He had not bathed or hardly changed clothes since he arrived. How could he forget to change clothes?

He immediately started giving away the supplies we brought in. We had worked hard to get these supplies on the flight, and he was handing them out to people with trucks to take to other camps. We stood back and watched until he started in on Martha and Kelly's medical cases. "Nope, those are for us to take care of the kids. We're stopping you here, Beaver."

First on our agenda was to hold the reins of the school so Sherrie would finally relent and fly back to the USA and get the medical attention she needed. I sat with her at the tiny airstrip where small private planes were circling waiting for their turn to land. She had scraps of cardboard with notes scribbled in crayons. The names of kids barely legible. "Check on this one, I think he might have a fracture. Make sure this one eats, she is still in shock. See if you can find this baby's momma. She has not shown up yet." All the notes to look after her kids. This wounded woman never stopped putting the kids ahead of her own needs.

Those weeks were filled with the absolute worst and best moments of humankind. The images and stories are etched into thousands of minds. I can say this one thing with confidence, the world came running to Haiti to help in any way she could. We met people from Uruguay and Paraguay, India and Turkey. Mexico came as well

as Canada. Haiti looked like the most beloved place on earth. That
was beautiful to me.

II. Moves, Mistakes and Messes

~ 8 ~

THE MOVE

"LIFE IS LIKE RIDING A BICYCLE.
TO KEEP YOUR BALANCE YOU MUST KEEP MOVING."
ALBERT EINSTEIN

In August of 2011, we finally made the full-time move to our beloved Haiti. We made the decision in March and started doing all the things one must do to leave life as you know it to begin in another place.

We painstakingly began to sell and give away our belongings. It was a sad show-closing Sunny Brooks Marketplace in Georgia. A friend offered to have an auction to help us. That's nice, I thought. Until I watched as people low-balled some of our most precious things. I was accustomed to being on the buying side of the auction. I had relished buying old cabinets for $10 only to bring them home, paint them up and resell for a profit. That was a thrill.

But to watch as others offered low bids for our precious old stuff was excruciating.

I remember one lady buying one of my grandmother's chairs--from her front room. This was a low-slung, sturdy wooden chair with cushions she had recovered herself how many times? With her own hands! This woman bid 5 dollars for it. 5 dollars! I couldn't bear it. I found her afterward and offered her 10 and bought it back.

Next, we turned our attention to our own home. This was another story altogether. Taking a lesson from the painful Marketplace liquidation sale, I left. I knew I could not bear watching people paying pennies for my beautiful rusty watering cans and creaky rocking chairs. Getting bargains on the tables where as a homeschool mom, I taught our daughter Rebecca to read or the stool Sam sat on to do the math. I couldn't do it.

So Rebecca and I packed up and went to Haiti for a month to work with our friends there. That was easier for me than to watch our sacred belongings indeed, some would say, junk, sold to strangers.

By August we were back in Georgia in a nearly empty house. Our sons had all moved into their own places over the previous few years and were working or in school. By the time we were ready to board the plane to Haiti as a family of three, we had gotten rid of most of our earthly belongings.

We allotted ourselves 3 suitcases each. But Rebecca, age 12, wasn't having it. It was the night before we were flying out and she still had not packed. Not a single item in her allotted 3 suitcases.

I don't think we realized our daughter was feeling quite so strongly about not leaving her beloved home and friends in the USA. In hindsight, I wish I had paid more attention to her unspoken hesitancy.

But instead, I said, girl, whatever is in those cases when we leave for the airport at 3 am, is what you will have to live with for the next 5 years. I can be so compassionate at times! Not my best parenting moment.

Fortunately, a dear friend came by and saved the day. She gave me a "I'll see what I can do" look and went into Rebecca's room with her, shutting the door behind them. It apparently worked. Girl had all her things of value in those cases and in the van at 3 am.

~ 9 ~

NOT RAISING THE DEAD

"HEAL THE SICK, RAISE THE DEAD"

MATTHEW 10:8

We moved to the town of Gonaives in August 2011. Pronounced "Go Naive". The name was fitting because we went in with so little understanding. It is the third-largest city in the nation and a three-hour drive north of the Capital city of Port Au Prince. We were drawn specifically into the sprawling, sun-drenched community of Jubilee on the edge of town. This community is The Picture of an impoverished developing world. Many of the houses are made from reclaimed scraps of tin, sticks, and mud. The more established families have concrete block walls here and there. Each day trucks overflowing with the city's garbage rumble past the tiny houses out into the narrowing strip of salt flats that separate these homes from the ocean. It is the literal end of the road.

We moved into a house, two miles from Jubilee, where friends that were soon to move back to the States had set up a big rooming house, formally a monastery for Catholic nuns. They were ready to depart and leave it with us. The house was a sort of base camp for people to come and work from, lovingly called "The Big House".

We stepped into the role we inherited as house parents. We were surrounded by beautiful, fierce, strongly determined young people who had also come from the US to live in the city and work in Jubilee. We were definitely the oldest in the group, but these young men and women became our closest friends and allies. We spent many hours dreaming together, focused on the community of Jubilee and how to make life better somehow for the people there.

Living in a community was like a red hot love affair. The passion of revolutionaries who were living sold out for a cause bigger than ourselves was intoxicating.

Together we walked through the garbage dump and rescued babies left there to die. We saw one find a family and thrive. We built a tiny coffin in the middle of the night from a wooden fish box, for the one that didn't make it. We drove madly through manifestations (roadblocks used to get the government's attention) to reach stranded visitors in the north. We drove through fire and had rocks hurled at us. It was incredible and bonding. And we had never felt so fully alive.

We applauded the teachers among us who got that one kid to finally write his name. We cried joy tears when a mother in the community saved her son from choking because she learned that skill in community health class earlier in the day. We celebrated every block room added to the building that housed the school and clinic. We showed up with paint and brushes and stayed till dark helping get it ready for kids the next day.

We wept and wailed and cussed and screamed at the night together when friends died or lost children to mystery deaths that came unexpectedly. I remember the first death of a child I experienced. We were called and when I got there I found Lala inside.

Laura Lynn Nichols, always and forever called Lala, is the director of the school in Jubilee. I often described her as a Barbie G.I. Joe. Think beautiful and tough! She is a no-nonsense, fierce lover of people.

When I got to the house where the child had died, LaLa was already there. We sat on the dirt floor in the tiny one-room house while the momma wailed her mourning wrapped in Lala's strong arms. I remember praying for the little girl to come back to life. I believed she would.

I hoped she would.

And then, I was afraid she would.

Cause what if she did? That would have a profound impact on several lives here.

I am not proud to tell you these thoughts. In other situations in the world where people don't sleep on dirt floors and children don't die unexpectedly for no reason, where churches are housed in buildings with padded chairs and nice carpet and consistent electricity. I was known as a woman of some faith. But in this world, my mind was reeling with the potential consequences if this child were to come back to life. She was very much no longer alive. Faith?

There were three possible unintentional outcomes:

1. She very likely could be treated like a zombie, abused, and cast out of her family circle. Zombie life is a real thing. Look it up if you want to go there.

2. Word would get out and people in the city would start to think we were somehow healers of all the dead. Would we be elevated to a deity and called to every single sickbed? (I know I sound like a terrible person for even having that thought. Don't judge, or you can. Either way, I was indeed thinking it.) The idea of my whole existence being known as a healer of all the dead and being dragged all over the city was not the way I imagined spending my days.

3. Or would it go the other way? Would we be accused of practicing magic powers? Would people want to stone us to death? Listen, you don't know what kind of questions your mind will come up with in these circumstances. We are taught in church and The Book tells us to raise the dead. It is pretty clear. But let me tell you. It has ramifications on the ground. It'll sober you up quickly.

But that didn't stop us from praying for her to rise, to come back, to breathe again. But she did not. She was the first person in Haiti I did not raise from the dead.

The second time I got one of those early morning phone calls I learned that one of our Artisans had died. Joseus. A man I knew well. A man I had seen the day before. A healthy man. A man whose wife had just given birth to their fifth beautiful child.

I threw on some clothes, cranked my little yellow motorcycle, and raced down to Jubilee to find a crowd in the road surrounding his house. In my mind, the crowd parted for me as I walked up. (But my mind does tend to dramatize things, so take that scene with a grain of salt.) Everyone knew he was an artisan who worked with us and I was at their home often sitting on the porch looking through pieces of metal and bringing bits of paper with new designs sketched on them. He smelted aluminum from the dump and made it into pendants for jewelry. We spent hours and hours together in the early days in his tiny grass hut of a workshop figuring out the process. Testing and retesting ideas. I was invested in this man and his family and I was not feeling this death.

Once again Lala had gotten there before me. His wife with her tear-stained face pushed back the curtain that was the door and let me in. It took a minute for my eyes to adjust to the dark room and then I saw him. His body was laid out on the floor on a sheet. He looked strong and healthy. He looked like he was just taking a nap.

I looked at Lala and she looked at me. Hell no, I thought. This isn't happening.

I squatted beside his still body and first prayed some good prayers. Jesus, please come. Please heal him. Please bring him back! We know you can. We know you died to give us life. Jesus pleeeeaaaassssseeee!

That didn't immediately work and I was well aware of my past failure at this attempt. So I paused. Then I tried another approach. I decided to take authority in the situation. We have authority, right? So I started pounding his chest... sort of a cross between CPR compressions that I had seen in movies and angry pounding. I chanted in unison to the beating: "live live live live live live live." I don't know how long we did this. I think Lala and I were both in on this part. She probably outlasted me as she is younger and stronger by far. This too failed to get a pulse or a breath.

Now I was just mad. I kept looking at his wife and the tiny ones that depended on him for their survival. No. Not happening. Not today, death. You can't have him.

Then I got loud. I began to tell him in no uncertain terms he was not leaving. Not now. His family needs him. We need him. I remember looking toward the corner of the room where the roof meets the wall. I had read stories of people with near-death experiences saying that they were looking down at their lifeless bodies trying to decide if they wanted to return or go toward the light. I said "Joseus, I know you are still around. You can't have gone far. Not yet. You need to forget about that light right now and come back here. Into this body." I went all boss lady on him.

He was young and strong and able. It was not his time to die. At least I didn't think so. His wife and kids didn't think so.

But he did. He did die. He didn't get up from his mat so we could make him some food. I wanted him to. But he did not.

This was the second person I did not raise from the dead. There are more. No one tells me I have "quite the anointing" anymore. And I guess that's ok.

~ 10 ~

COMPOSTING 101

"PRIDE IS THE MOTHER OF ARROGANCE."
TOBA BETA

I remember well a conversation that took place about four months after we moved to Haiti.

I found myself in a nice restaurant sitting at a big round table in Petionville, a wealthy area of Port au Prince. We drove the 3 hours down from Gonaives to drop a mission team at the airport and needed to stay a night in the city to pick up another group the next day. In those early years this was part of our routine. Visitors nearly weekly.

But here I was about to eat as much food as I possibly could. The gentleman to my right, one of the "new to me" people was somewhat of a legend in the world of nonprofit work. He had been a consultant in Haiti for many years. Smart person with all the language of someone who actually does real research before he acts.

While we waited on our egg rolls he politely turned to me and asked, *What work are you doing here in Haiti?* I was ready.

You see when we landed in Jubilee the existence of real hunger in real people smacked me upside my American "I always need to lose weight" face. I discovered that there is a palpable sensation of hunger in the atmosphere where there are many bodies in need of energy. It's like there is a caloric vacuum in the air. And though I was quick to hand out small money for food to whoever asked, it was not long before my small chunk of change ran low.

Then I had a brilliant idea. I'll teach everyone here to plant gardens in their own yards and grow their own food! That will solve the hunger problem.

There were a few minor problems with my idea. I'm going to take some ink and lay them out for you one humiliating point at a time.

1st Problem

Jubilee is a salt flat. The dirt is literally made of a huge concentration of salt. It even seeps up into the concrete floors after a good rain. It is a great place to harvest salt. That is probably why there are over 50 salt ponds there where people are doing that exact thing. There is not a tree or bush or flower or blade of grass across most of this land. It simply is not the right soil.

No problem, I thought. Not for this white girl. We can make our own soil! Compost! It's the trending idea among homeschool families in the USA and I can teach all the people how to do it, she thought as she quickly Googled, "How to compost." Because of course, I had never actually composted a thing in my life.

So after my extensive research (three articles, thank you Google), I decided to build a community compost system. My "Step Number One" to ending hunger in Jubilee. I chose an empty spot in the middle of the community. There was an old toilet center there. Is that the right name? What else do you call a little concrete house built in the middle of the salt flat with three stalls to go in and do your business? These had been built by a previous NGO and within a short time were so utterly disgusting, due to serious design flaws, so that no one would use them. The community asked if, before I began my *compost trick*, if we would brick it up because it stunk and was ugly. So that became the first step to composting: Block up the toilet center.

Then I hired someone to help me dig three small pits so that the compost could be tossed and turned. Google gave me very specific instructions as to the percentage of paper to fiber to vegetables to fruit peels. I could tell it was going to take some time to get it down just right, but I was not deterred.

The blocked-up toilet center came in very handy as now I had a big flat surface on which to paint. I had the instructions for proper composting translated into Kreyol and I proceeded to make a beautiful compost instruction mural on the side of the toilet center facing the pits. It was a little bare so I added some nice palm trees too.

I drew quite the crowd out there in my overalls and box of paints. I knew nothing about crowd control or saying no when teenage boys picked up my paints and walked off. I had no idea how to respond when a lady challenged me as to why I didn't come to paint her house next. Back then I was so green. I had some make-believe idea that I was different from "them". That I had to prove something to show "them" love. That I was bringing Christ to a place that He wasn't already! Oh my! How that makes me cringe. I had bought the White Savior mentality hook, line and sinker and it would soon crush me.

But we eventually got the compost instructions painted on the defunct toilet center. We got the three pits dug so that our compost would be orderly and flippable. We paid for dozens and dozens of sticks and built a fence to surround it with a couple of real pieces of wood to make the gate. What could go wrong?

2nd Problem

I never stopped to ask who the land belonged to. I just picked an empty spot in the middle of the garbage and salty dirt and started. What horror I felt when I drove in one morning to find out that the local magistrate/pastor was furious. He was small but scary as heck. He wanted to know where I got the authority to work on that piece of land. My first thought was to bow up and use all my white girl savior attitude.

I am doing all this hard work for you guys. How can you question me using this tiny piece of land that was covered in garbage and not being used anyway?

Then, thankfully before those arrogant words spilled out of my mouth, I got a check from that same Wise Voice.

Girl, what are you doing? You know you should have asked first. Go find the man, humble yourself, beg his forgiveness, explain what you are thinking, and ask for his advice.

It worked and we made up. I got permission and he welcomed me to continue. Looking back, I can't even imagine the laughter the community must have enjoyed at my expense! Of course he let me keep going. It was good entertainment.

3rd Problem

There were no scraps. Zero. No leftovers scraped off plates after dinner is done. Not even a single grain of rice is left in the pot that cooked it. There is no evening newspaper to add to get the percentage of fiber to greens just right. There was nothing. Nada. *Anyen.*

For weeks my beautiful fenced-in pits waiting for scraps sat empty. Then finally I think the community felt sorry for me and someone dumped orange and *sitwon* peelings in the pit. I was so happy. I was happy dancing arms in the air. Ok. It's going to work now. Here we go.

I came back the next day and it looked like Armageddon had happened. In the night the pigs and goats had smashed down the sticks that had been the fence to get to their food. What had been our neat piles of peels waiting to become dirt were now only shreds of orange and green. Everyone knows peels are for pigs. I had built a very fancy food trough.

4th Problem

Weeks later the rainy season started and I learned what everyone else in the community knew all along. There was a reason there were no houses built on that spot. I had chosen the lowest ground and the whole thing was under water. End of story. End of compost project. Temporary End of white girl arrogance.

Back at the fancy restaurant in Petionville, I responded to the man's question with an air of confidence **I should not have had**.

I am starting a composting project so that the people in the community can grow their own food.

Him: Why?
Me: Umm. Because there is not enough food, and people are hungry. (Duh, man)

Him: There is not enough food? (Note this was said in a kind of snarky tone)
Me: Well, Clearly, I said. (Jeez, maybe this guy is not as smart as we think. Maybe he is out of touch with the "real Haiti". Clearly there is not enough food because people are practically starving.)

Him: Have you seen any of the local markets since you moved here? Perhaps you drive past one in your town?
Me: Well of course I have, I said. Or thought. (This question made me a little nervous)

Him: Did you see baskets full of tomatoes and eggplant and onions and rice and oranges and pineapple and potatoes and greens and bananas and bread and all the other things people eat?
Me: Umm. Yes, now that you mention it the market does seem to be quite full.

Him: What the people need is jobs. So they can buy the food from farmers. (who actually KNOW what they're doing, he thought to himself but was too refined to say it out loud)

If I could have slid down my chair and under the rug, I would have done it.

Yeah, that's what I meant, I thought. I am going to start a business so people can have jobs and real paychecks and buy food from farmers who actually know how and where to grow it. That's what I meant, right?

~ 11 ~

REPEATED HUMILIATIONS TO
THE EGO

"GROWTH HAPPENS AS A RESULT OF REPEATED
HUMILIATIONS TO THE EGO"
-CARL JUNG

I have learned that moving to a foreign land is, if nothing else, a series of "repeated humiliations to the ego." We leave the U.S. thinking we are technologically advanced people, full of life experiences and education that make us so smart. We land in a developing world and realize pretty quickly, almost none of that smartness is going to help. Haitians have a proverb for this which basically says, if you don't take care of the foreigners, they won't last a day. It is so true. We don't have a clue how to do life here.

Language is the first source of cluelessness. Being in a room full of people and having virtually no idea what is going on is humiliating at its best. Dangerous at its worst. Especially when everyone is laughing and you feel like you should laugh, too. But you aren't sure because it is likely they are laughing at you!

I would love to share stories of my early days when we first began working in Haiti and I had little vocabulary. But my stories are more recent. It seems I have learned and practiced enough Kreyol to appear fluent in good moments. And to remain clueless in others.

For instance, I would be talking with Mafie, a coworker and dear friend I have known since the beginning, about something to do with a necklace design. And we'd be doing fine until Christella walked in the room and she and Mafie began a whole other conversation about what, I could not tell you. I could only understand an odd word they'd say to one another! It could be that she was telling her that she was leaving because someone in her family died or she could be telling her she is leaving to go pick up lunch. I didn't know. I was lost. I would just stand there like the idiot I was.

I used to really work at it and study vocabulary words every night. Now, I have come to the place of saying, I have come halfway, people. I am old. You are young. You guys can learn a bit of English!

This is a horrible attitude, I know. But my brain is tired.

And then there are those occasions when only Kreyol will come from my mouth.

I found this out one time when I was as sick as a human ever needs to be. So sick I think I slept in the shower for a couple of days. There was so much pouring out of my body, it was easier just to stay in there. Gross, I know. Forgive me for speaking of such realities. But you should know it took four bags of IV fluid to get me to pee.

(That is how we measure our sicknesses here. How many bags did you need? It is kind of a sick source of pride.) In those hours of utter pain and weakness, I only spoke Kreyol. And mostly phrases like, "Jezi! Ed m" Jesus! Help me!

It also seems to come to me spontaneously when I get really angry. Which makes sense because Kreyol is a full body language. It comes with hand signals and clicks of the mouth and a cool sucking-the-teeth thing. It is great for expressing outrage. "O mon Cher!" Imagine hands flipping up and a good teeth suck.

It is also the language for prayer. I find when I get lost in prayer, really get to the high places, I often switch into Kreyol. Maybe my soul secretly knows that God plays favorites after all and the Haitian people are near the top of his list!

But the really embarrassing thing I do, and it always makes my daughter cringe when she hears it, is when I am in the USA, I spontaneously speak Kreyol to ALL children and all brown and black-bodied people. I literally have to force my lips to form English words, even with my own grandchildren. It is strange, strange, strange.

Which is not fair because I am clearly not truly fluent. As much as some people like to say that I am, I know the truth! And I have learned the hard way it is better to not guess what people are saying. I have caused way too many problems trying to hide my ignorance by shaking my head yes as if I understand.

For example, an artisan came to me to explain a problem.

This is what I heard:

"My mother is sick and needs an operation on her head. I am going to take three days off work to take her to the hospital and then to the countryside so she can rest. I will be back on Friday."

This is what she said:

"We need to order three rolls of fabric to finish the top of the Momma Totes if we are going to get these bags ready for Friday."

So you can see how this could be a problem? Now I make sure I bring a person who can translate exactly what is being said into any deep conversations. I have embraced humility like an old ridiculously dressed aunt. She, Humility, comes with me no matter what anyone thinks. I am too old for this nonsense of trying to look smarter than I am.

~ 12 ~

TRASH AND TRUST

"TO BE TRUSTED IS A GREATER COMPLIMENT THAN BEING LOVED."
GEORGE MACDONALD

You should know this about me. I am no great artist. But I am one of the most creative souls you will likely ever meet. I am not proud of this. I can't even help it. It is my genetic flow. It's like I have a hundred children inside my head crying to make stuff all day every day. But because of this, I can pretty much make something out of anything. Give me some twine, scissors, garbage, or ocean, and leave me alone for a minute. This mentality served me well in a seaside community built beside the dump.

In the early days, a friend came to visit. She brought tools to make jewelry. We gathered the women, about 30 of them, and she taught classes for a week. We scavenged colorful pieces of broken glass, washed and sanded the edges, wrapped them in wire, and made our first pendants. We made earrings and necklaces with only minor cuts along the way. At the end of it, she left us her tool kit. I wonder if she ever imagined how far her gift would take us? 2nd Story Goods makers are using these skills to this day.

I had a hard time convincing the women to find the treasures in the trash. Although there is a whole fleet of kids and old people that were known to be scavengers, it was generally looked down upon. There is great pride here. So I just did it. I walked around with my burlap bag gathering up treasures. Round pieces of glass, a cork, sticks of metal, a bent spoon, shells, and bottle caps. I'd sit down in the half-finished school room and take out the twine and wire and start wrapping. Slowly the women gathered around. They mostly sat around and talked crap about me in their secret language I had yet to decode. The young women would join me first. Wriggling into the room and making a spot beside me on the floor.

I wish I still had some of those early wind chimes of trash. Some of my best art no doubt. Eventually, even the pastor's wife laid her pride aside and picked up the treasures, and started on her own work. She had been the most vocal in questioning my sanity. We all laughed hard and loud when she lowered herself to join us on the concrete slab.

The first few years, yes years, were about building relationships and trust. I spent a lot of time walking around in the mud and trash asking the divine Voice who to talk to and which way to turn. I repeat I knew nothing.

I remember distinctly when I realized I needed to find the true leader in the group of women. There were a lot of strongly opinionated women in the group. It seemed like no matter how clear I tried to be there was always a big loud fight at the end of the week when it was time to collect work and pay people. I needed someone I could explain things to one on one and who in turn could help others to understand. I was scared. I was still unaccustomed to the loudness of conversations in this culture. I was a quiet white woman who thought that maintaining a calm peaceful composure in the face of all combative discussion is the true win. This culture couldn't be more opposite to that thought. I was pretty much terrified every Friday.

A lot of the fights and yelling broke out over money. For those of you that don't know, there is this imaginative way of counting money in Haiti. Imaginative in that it seems like a plot of the most sinister kind.

The official currency is the Haitian Gourde. But there is this UNofficial thing called the Haitian Dollar. It has something to do with US Marines landing here. It is confusing because when someone gives a price of 100, you must clarify. Otherwise, you don't know if they mean 100 Gourdes (about 1 USD) or 100 Haitian Dollars (roughly 5 USD). Even if you say it clearly that you are speaking in Gourds, among those most marginalized and least educated, there is only one way of thinking about the bills. As when you hold a 100 HTG (official currency Haitian Gourde) bill some people will only be able to tell you it is 20 Haitian dollars. They grew up hearing their mothers and everyone around them refer to that 100 Haitian Gourde Bill as 20 dollars. If that is what you've known in your home and your community your entire life, that is what it is. The word one hundred is never uttered. So when someone tells you that your work is worth 20 HTG, they see in their heads the bill that clearly is marked 100 HTG. Because that is what they have always known to be 100 dollars.

Clear as mud, right?

And the thing is you never know exactly what the person is thinking. I was new to the idea of calling something by a name other than what it was marked. My gosh, I had only just learned to pronounce all the numbers in Kreyol!

I can't begin to tell you how confusing this gets at the most basic level. Hence a lot of yelling and threatening gestures and terror, like for my life. I could not imagine that these women would think I was somehow wanting to cheat them. How could that enter their minds when what I wanted to do more than anything was give them money?

When it comes to money, jobs, and resources in general there is little trust.

Social Capital is defined as "those factors of effectively functioning **social** groups that include such things as interpersonal relationships, a shared sense of identity, a shared understanding, shared norms, shared values, trust, cooperation, and reciprocity."

Haiti is strong in a shared sense of identity and a shared understanding. But the huge division of wealth and the history of the poor consistently being left out of the equation when it comes to using the country's resources means no one believes anyone is going to do something for the community's best interest. It is an uphill battle.

And it is one that is shocking to most of us that come here feeling as if we have given up our easy cushy hot water and air-conditioned lives to live without electricity and ice. We find it hard to realize that after the shiny wears off, people don't trust us. Why should they really? It takes time.

So I prayed to find an ally. To find the leader in this group of strong personalities. Who would it be? So many fierce women. I had narrowed it down to three of them. And was leaning toward one. I was about to travel for a week and I needed to leave supplies and money with someone. When I asked a few people who I should leave it with they all gave the same response. Mafie.

Yes. Found our leader. Not the loudest one.

But the respected one.

~ 13 ~

PERSPECTIVE

"IN ALL AFFAIRS IT'S A HEALTHY THING NOW AND THEN TO HANG A
QUESTIONMARK ON THE THINGS YOU HAVE LONG TAKEN FOR
GRANTED."
BERTRAND RUSSELL

It's probably pretty clear by now, but if not, let me say it again. I had no idea what I was doing. And my Today Self would tell my 2011 Self this is unacceptable. We can do real harm when we're out here all kamikaze. We make mistakes. These are real lives and real cities that we're messing with. Because we come in with financial backing, we can unintentionally upset the balance of communities and make the wrong people leaders with the flip of our well-resourced wands. It is a tense line to walk. This knowing what to do with our financial resources.

I found this entry in my journal from those early days:

"I can't help it. Honestly, I love this. And I hate this, too. I love the environment of life all raw and real and in my face. I love the passion involved in buying a stalk of bananas and arguing over pennies in the deal. I love walking over the salt flats and mud to get to the sea to watch wooden fishing boats pull in their nets. I love visiting the mamas in their homes as they show me each of their children with pride."

I loved the life-changing projects of the school, the garden, the training, and the jobs.

But I hated the role I often found myself in.

The White Lady. The one whose pockets never ran empty.

The fact that in the midst of working on big projects, I was greeted many times each day with *"I am hungry. My children are hungry. You give me food. Give me sandals. Give me tennis shoes. I need you to give me money for school, for a funeral, to go visit my sick dad, for water... to buy soap to wash my clothes and my baby's clothes. I need you to pay this or that for me."*

These were often sincere, real needs. And we helpers with our stateside support had taught this people group to ask us.

And Jesus had the audacity to say it too. "Give to those who ask."

Really? Had he been here?

It is tough. I'm not going to lie. I loved it here, but I didn't love the many times a day I faced the situation of this person before me, desperate for something.

And I felt like, yes, you and I both know that I could reach for my bag and produce the money to make this better for you. And you. And you.

But where did I draw the line? Because every time I tried to draw one the dust blew in and rendered it useless.

Do unto others as you would have them do unto you. That is a pretty cut and dry formula. And it helped in a lot of cases. Especially when I knew the people and knew that their needs were authentic.

But what about the other 25 requests each day? I tried to put myself in their shoes (or non-shoes). How could I help without becoming the "white-lady-has-money" answer to every problem?

It is not something I heard missionaries talk about a lot. But the ones I talked to here admitted it was a daily struggle.

I can't feel good about starting a White Lady Movement that convinces the community that I have all the resources that will ever be needed. Nor can I feel good about saying no to everyone who asks.

Maybe "yes" for Monday, Wednesday, and Friday and "no" the other days?

And as I struggled through I heard this:

You think being the "Asked" is difficult?
Would you like to swap places with the ones asking?

Perspective.

~ 14 ~

COURAGEOUS POT MAKING 101

"MAKING THE SIMPLE COMPLICATED IS COMMONPLACE; MAKING THE
COMPLICATED SIMPLE, AWESOMELY SIMPLE, THAT'S CREATIVITY."
CHARLES MINGUS

By 2011 I was still wandering around Jubilee, praying under my breath the most astute of all prayers.

Help!

One day as I wandered, I and a small band of local teenagers visited a man that makes aluminum cooking pots for a living. He has a humble thatch hut on the very outskirts of Jubilee. His domain is easily identifiable by the black soot that surrounds the ground where he works.

We found this sinewy man. (Though he appeared ancient, in truth I was likely his senior by at least five years. It dawned on me that maybe I also appeared ancient!?) He was stoking the fire that burned hot, fueled by a strip of old tire. Tires burn well. But the fumes are horrible.

I watched as he uncovered the chamber holding the melting aluminum cans and stirred to see if the liquid was ready. Though we spoke and he answered patiently, he seemed to be completely unmoved by this crowd of teenagers and one white lady that had come to visit.

Watching him silently meticulously working his craft, stirred my soul. Makers doing their making always does.

We peered into the simple thatch building where he had wooden frames laid out on the dirt floor. The fine dirt held the forms for the liquid metal to be cast, he explained. Again, silently, with confidence, he worked, skimming the dirt gently at first, then pounding it down until it was ready.

In all this wandering, I was searching - Always seeking ways to create products that would create jobs. July and August were the months that intensified the scramble. Every day as the official opening date for the government schools drew near, more parents asked for help to pay school fees. The kids themselves asked for help too; they were desperate to stay in school. It was a great privilege to have uniforms and books and a place to report to each day to learn.

So I prayed more "help" prayers. I tried to imagine business plans that would work with molten metal. This is way before I realized I needed to do more than come up with jewelry ideas... way before I understood that we needed to build an actual company. The company that was to become 2nd Story Goods.

And how could we do that here in Jubilee where there is no running water or at that time, electricity. I wondered how we could push forward for a way of life that was beyond the daily acceptance of things like diarrhea that kills, unsafe housing, and crippling mindsets. The mountain of problems that were a part of daily existence left little room for creative big-picture problem-solving.

At this point in our visit, one of the young men in our entourage picked up one of the finished pots stacked loosely in the mud at our feet and said:

" I love Jesus" and I said, "What?"

He pointed to the side of each pot. The man has 'engraved' I (heart) Jesus on each piece. I was stunned!

I asked, **HOW** do you get the impression in the mold of the pots? Thinking, if we put words on aluminum pieces, Wow! That opens up serious possibilities!

So I asked again, how? How did you get the words in there? He turned slowly, looking at this strange white woman who all of a sudden seemed so very excited. With the patience of an old soul, he answered that he used a *"Bouwèt"*.

Ok, I knew the word *Bouwèt* meant wheelbarrow. So I began to try to figure out the correlation between a wheelbarrow and this small stamp. Hmm? Did he use a part from a wheelbarrow? Did he cut up the side and make a mold? How did he do this magic? I was scanning the ground looking for clues.

Finally, I gave up. I had to wait until there was a break in the activity of his work. He did not slow down or skip a step in his process just because we were there watching.

I waited patiently. Actually, I waited impatiently. Then asked, "Can you show me how you did it?" I was prepared to stand for the next hour as he took us through the arduous process he went through to get this clean impression on the side of his cooking pots.

I watched wide-eyed, pen in hand, ready to take notes, as he slowly reached into his pocket and pulled out a small plastic pink hair clasp that some people call a barrette. This one says I (heart) Jesus.

Yep.

Barret, not **Bouwèt,** smart white lady.

Then he went long into a description of not **HOW** he put this impression on the pots, but rather, **WHY** he put the impression in the mold. Because this is what he really wanted white lady to understand. Not HOW but WHY.

"Jesus is the one who gives me the courage to keep going. Jesus only," the courageous Pot Maker said.

He smiled a deeply authentic smile and nodded his knowing head at me. And I felt like he knew a bunch more than I did. I felt like he was trying to remind me. And I kind of got it. "Take courage Jezi leads you. Keep going Jezi is with you. Keep walking through the garbage and the mud. Keep seeking. Keep knocking. You can't see it yet, dear sister, but keep going, you will."

This is what it looked like on the ground for me in those days. Wandering in the garbage and mud. Messy and beautiful. This guy preached me a good sermon that day. He and his barrette.

~ 15 ~

ANITE

"IT IS NOT UNTIL YOU BECOME A MOTHER THAT YOUR JUDGMENT
SLOWLY TURNS TO COMPASSION AND UNDERSTANDING."

ERMA BOMBECK

Anite is one of the women that joined the 2nd Story Goods tribe in the early years.

One day I watched her face as she sewed. She worked with such intensity. There was a heavy calm there. As if she had mastered the art of carrying the weight of her heavy world on her tiny shoulders.

I first met Anite when the nurses brought her to our tiny atelier/ workshop, otherwise known as the small one-room house we rented in Jubilee for this work.

This particular day two amazing young women, the "American nurses" walked in casually, with sweet smiles on their faces. Which let me know they were up to something! Ha! "Hey, Mama k. We'd like you to meet this wonderful mom, Anite. We're wondering if you might have work for her?"

This was the general relationship between all of us immigrants (some call us missionaries, but I like immigrants). If I had a momma with a child that needed to get into school I'd call Lala at the Jubilee School. If Lala had a student who was sick, she'd call the nurses. If the nurses had a momma that needed work, they'd call me. It was a cycle of using each other and it worked out well most of the time!

In her arms, this tiny woman, Anite, carried her 5-year-old son, born with a condition called Hydrocephalus, sometimes referred to as water on the brain. It is a condition where fluid builds up in the brain cavities because there is something that is keeping it from draining. Most often either surgery can correct it or a shunt can be put in to let the fluid drain out elsewhere, like to the stomach. Sometimes if the shunt doesn't work right and the pressure continues it can cause the head to swell really large. These kids then suffer with bad headaches, and sometimes even brain damage and painful seizures.

This is what happened to Anite's son. He was suffering. He had seen the surgeons in Port Au Prince. But he was not getting better.

But he was getting loved! His momma Anite loved and protected him fiercely. He had beautiful brown eyes with the longest eyelashes and his whole face lit up when he smiled. Which was often. But he was painfully thin. All skin and bones. I lifted him from her arms, so she could pick up the patch and needle and thread held out to her.

I was stunned by his weight, his body so frail, yet with the extra fluids on his brain, he was so very heavy. How did this tiny woman carry this child all over town? She couldn't be an ounce over 75 pounds herself.

Here in this culture, people are often superstitious about kids born with special needs. There are rumors of them being devil kids or somehow less than fully human. I could only imagine the shaming and derision this young mom had experienced in the past 5 years, carrying this child in her arms.

Can you sew? I asked her.
"Yes"

Can you come sew this for us to see?
"Ok"

I held my breath, not knowing how the ladies in the sewing group sitting all around the room, watching, would respond to her and her son.

They might go low and taunt her or make unkind remarks about her son. Or they could go high and welcome her in as they tried to understand her predicament. Back then, in those days I never knew how it would go.

To my relief, they went high! It was lovely the way they welcomed her. And him. After some honest questions about his condition and their life, they handed her another patch, showed her how to place the tags together, and welcomed her into our tiny, close-knit circle. My heart nearly burst with gratitude that they did this. These women could be hard and judge, but they chose soft and accepting instead. They widened the circle and brought her in.

She hand-stitched two small pieces of fabric together -- the "tags" we added to all our bags. They said DIGNITY. POSSIBILITIES. PEACE. HOPE. This seemed right, so right, that she took this job.

Her son was the youngest of four children. His father died or went missing during the flood in Gonaives in 2008. She had raised four children on her own.

Looking way back in my own life, I remember when our first four sons were young. They were healthy and walking. I had electricity, a washing machine, running water, easy food, a secure house, a vehicle, and a husband to share the load and hold me in his arms and make me feel loved and beautiful even when I was exhausted and whiney.

I had ALL THE THINGS. And it was hard.

But Anite, she did not. And I was in awe of her.

For months after that initial meeting, she came by each week and delivered the pieces she had taken home to sew. We would pay her for her work and reload her with more tags. After a bit she began to come and sit awhile, enjoying the sweet camaraderie in our warm little sewing room, before she headed back home, her tiny purse bulging with a bit of cash, and more work to be done.

I feel certain that employing Anite was one of the most important things I have done in my life. And looking at it from the outside in, it was so, so, so small.

One day I gave her a ride home. At that time she lived in town. I parked my small motorcycle on the street and we walked through a very narrow alley, behind a nice block-built house into a small courtyard where it appeared a few families were living together.

She showed me her space and then confided in me that she had to move. The landlord had let her stay in one of the tiny 10 x 8-foot sheds in the courtyard for a time. But it had become a troubling situation. Now they wanted her out and she felt her kids were unsafe. She told me she wanted to move into Jubilee with them.

What? I really questioned her on this. Jubilee is not for the faint of heart! It is the social, economical, and literal end of the road in our city. It is a salt flat where there is virtually no green. It is the place where the city trucks dump the garbage load after load, setting the piles on fire before they drive away. It is where many people live, but only because it is their last option.

As it was, the previous week we lost Mafie's precious sister who was also a part of our jewelry-making group. After a year-long fight, she lost the battle with immune deficiency disorder. She left behind her two girls and her tiny rock house in Jubilee. The family was selling it to pay for the funeral expense.

So we bought the house enabling Mafie and her family to bury her sister. And we gave the house to Anite so she could raise her tiny family in peace. The great sadness mingled into a thread of joy and gratitude.

We prayed for new patterns of grace and compassion to grow in the neighborhood so that Anite and her tiny family could survive and begin to thrive in this place. She had faith for that. I visited her many many times in that house. Eventually, she made enough money to put in a private toilet in the backyard so that her girls didn't have to relieve themselves out in the garbage piles. She wanted them safe.

A year later her beautiful son passed away. And all I can say is that he was loved. He was able to live his short life with his mom and sisters that adored him.

I know we get so many things wrong. But I believe we got this one right.

III. Change the
Question

~ 16 ~

CHANGE THE QUESTION

"THE WIFE OF A MAN FROM THE COMPANY OF
THE PROPHETS CRIED OUT TO ELISHA,
"YOUR SERVANT MY HUSBAND IS DEAD, AND YOU
KNOW THAT HE REVERED THE LORD.
BUT NOW HIS CREDITOR
IS COMING TO TAKE MY TWO BOYS AS HIS SLAVES.
"ELISHA REPLIED TO HER, "HOW CAN I HELP YOU? TELL ME,
WHAT DO YOU HAVE IN YOUR HOUSE?"
2 KINGS 4:1-2

Reading one morning in the sacred text I came across the familiar story in 2 Kings 4 of a poor widow who finds herself in crisis and goes to the local missionary/prophet and explains her situation.

Working in Jubilee, this was a familiar story to me. I heard it several times a month. Desperate mom, rent was due and she had no way to pay it so she was about to lose her home and her kids. So I read this familiar passage as I've never read it before. It had my FULL attention.

The widow comes to the prophet with her impossible situation. Needing help. Needing to be rescued. Needing some cold hard cash. But what does he say? How does he respond to this desperate situation?

He asks her, "Lady, what do you HAVE?"

This! This is how you reply to a widow in need? This is what you say to someone in a dire situation? This!?!?

What do you **HAVE**?

I'm thinking, dang. Man's got some kind of nerve! Because the only question I was asking day and night was, WHAT do you need? What do YOU need? What do you NEED? All the ways to ask the same thing.

But never this question. Never, What do you HAVE!

I read on.

And she replies, "Nothing."

I can hear the Haitian mamma say it. *Pa gen anyen.* The Kreyol way of saying, *I have nothing,* as she slaps the backs of her hands to her palms. Over and under. The universal sign for Anyen. Empty. I got nothing.

And then these few cautious words slip out of her mouth.

"Except I do have a tiny smidgen of oil."

Great! I can practically see the prophet's face light up with too much hope. An explosion of joy. You DO have something. More importantly, you can SEE that you do have something. And we can work with that.

"Here's what you do," said Elisha. "Go up and down the street and borrow empty jugs and bowls from all your neighbors. And not just a few—all you can get. Then come home and lock the door behind you, you and your sons. Pour oil into each container; when each is full, set it aside.

She did what he said. She locked the door behind her and her sons; as they brought the containers to her, she filled them. When all the jugs and bowls were full, she said to one of her sons, "Another jug, please." He said, "That's it. There are no more jugs." Then the oil stopped. She went and told the story to the man of God. He said, "Go sell the oil and make good on your debts. Live, both you and your sons, on what's left."

I'd like to point out a few things here:

1. Point for the missionary/helper/prophet person. This is not an easy question to ask of someone in need. It does not make them adore you or depend on you or include you in their testimony of how their life was changed. Other fellow helpers can misunderstand you or judge you or call you selfish. It happens.

2. Point for the widow. She had to have eyes to see that she did have something. I am a firm believer that the economy of heaven is both abundant and at the same time never wasteful. Extravagant and Responsible. Seems we need to use what we have before receiving more. And we can't use what we have if we don't see and admit that we have it. She saw.

3. Point for the kindness of heaven. A mom's greatest terror is losing a child. Can you even imagine how terrified this mom was when the authorities were threatening to take her sons and make them slaves until she could pay her debt? Being a mom of many,

I know that that threat throws your psyche into a whole new universe. It is the last thing.

I love the way the story is so particular to point out that he said:

"Then come home and lock the door behind you, you and your sons.

Pour oil into each container; when each is full, set it aside."

Instead of losing them, they were pulled in close and started a family business together! Oh, how I love this!

4. Another point for the widow. She listened to the advice. And she took it. She didn't give up. She threw herself into action. What faith! Surely the neighbors shook their heads, whispering "bless her heart" as they watched the drama play out. She looked a little unhinged collecting her neighbors' empty Tupperware containers but she did it anyway.

And the result? The oil couldn't help itself. It multiplied in that environment. I think that is the way of heaven. Standing on tiptoe at all times waiting for an opening. Any tiny opening to pour into. The woman cracked open the door and the sweet ways of heaven rushed in. She filled all the containers. Sold them back to her community and paid her debt.

She then launched her own Oil Business, hired several single moms franchised to Egypt, and sent her sons to good schools in Mesopotamia. Maybe I embellished that part a bit!

The big takeaway from this story for me is that when we change the question from what do you need to what do you have, it flips everything.

It shows respect. It acknowledges that everyone has something.

I think it is the single most important thing I have learned.

And I think it is a critical piece for the world of helpers and the helped today.

Until we as helpers understand that the person across the table from us needing help has something of value to bring to the equation,we will most likely do harm with our helping.

Please understand I do not mean when we are doing relief work after an earthquake or storm. In those situations we are giving, giving, giving! Generously, quickly and with great intention.

I am talking about communities that exist in systemic poverty, in generational situations of perpetual need.

We must begin to change the question.
From: What do you need?
To: What do you have?

~ 17 ~

HOW TO KEEP POOR PEOPLE POOR

"WHEN I DISCOVER WHO I AM, I'LL BE FREE."
RALPH ELLISON

One day, I was traveling with Benson to Port Au Prince in the car to buy supplies. Just me and him. Benson Thermidor is the leader of the Leather Workshop. He has grown it from a one-man operation binding songbooks and recovering Bibles to a company employing nearly twenty people. Now they make journals and leather bags that have become the centerpiece of 2nd Story Goods.

I came to love these one-on-one times in the car with this young brilliant person. First, he would sleep for an hour, but after that, I could count on him for some great conversation. So I got to where I would pull out my phone and ask,

Is it ok for me to record our conversation?

Then I hit record when he started talking.

One day we were driving along and he said to me:

Mk, do you know how to keep poor people poor?

No, Benson, I don't. I can't say I have ever had a reason to think about that question. How do you keep poor people poor?

Give them everything they need.

I thought to myself: This is going to be interesting. He continued:

Give them food and clothes and houses. Give it to them and never ask them to do anything for it. Do this for a long time. Year after year. That way they never develop their own capacity. That way they never grow and they will always need you. They will stay dependent on you.

I thought to myself, I sure wish I was recording this right now. He is in full teacher mode and I didn't want to miss a thing.

Mk, do you realize that when you met me as a young man, you saw that I came from a poor family with many brothers and sisters. You could have decided to help me by bringing us clothes and food and paying our bills each month. You could have just seen our lack, instead of seeing me as a young man with great capacity. If you had done that, where would I be today?

Where would I be today? He asked again. *I would not know my capacity to build a company and make beautiful products like this,* (pointing to the Leather Bags in the back seat.) *I would not be who I am today, a leader in my community and a provider for my family.*

The day I met him he had approached me on the salt flats. By this time word was getting around that there was a Blanc (foreigner) in

the area looking for things to be made here. He approached me re-
spectfully and said,

Madam, I would like to show you something.

Thank Heaven I didn't blow him off. Thank Heaven I paused long
enough to see. Thank heaven *this time* I did that.

He then reached into his backpack and pulled out a black vinyl-
covered book. The outside had designs made with rhinestones and
an inlaid picture of the palace in Port Au Prince. I opened it up to
see what sort of book he had recovered. It was a journal of empty
pages. And the pages were sewn into the binder with great care. It
was perfect and marketable, except for the rhinestones and picture
of the palace part.

So I asked him where he got it. He said he made it. I looked at the
careful binding again. You MADE this? You sewed these papers together like this

Yes. Yes, I did. Would you like to buy it? Or buy many of them?

I paused a minute and asked where he lived. Close by, two streets
over, he said.

Can you teach others to do this? I asked.

We gathered up money and created a small contract to have him
teach an 8-week class to some of the women in the community. I
also enrolled in that first class. I too wanted to learn the art of journal making. It was fascinating and really hard. There are a lot of
fractions involved!

I loved watching him one day trying to convey the idea of fractions to women who had missed that part of school. They could not imagine something smaller than one whole. I watched him pause and think.

And then he turned the whole thing into a money problem using the local currency, which every woman in the class had been handling one way or another since childhood. They instantly got it!

I wrote in my journal that day, real big: THIS KID IS BRILLIANT.

I still believe it.

~ 18 ~

BUILD A HIGHWAY, REMOVE
THE STONES

"PEOPLE OF JERUSALEM, OPEN YOUR GATES! REPAIR THE ROAD TO

THE CITY AND CLEAR IT OF STONES;

RAISE A BANNER TO HELP THE NATIONS FIND THEIR WAY."

ISAIAH 62:10

Meet the young potters of 2nd Story Goods.

They travel over a hundred miles to the place where the best heavy dirt is found for making clay. Local people harvest it from the river and sell it to makers. Our potters then hire a truck and haul the 100 lb bags of clay back to Gonaives, a 3-hour drive. Then once here, they unload the impossibly heavy bags in the outdoor workshop where we work.

Little by little, they add the clay dirt to water and stir it with a sturdy board in a 55-gallon drum until it is rehydrated. Next, they push it through a mesh screen and then a porous cloth to purify it. Afterward, they lay it out to dry and then pound it into balls of workable substance. This takes days. Eventually, they form it and throw it on our not quite right electric/not electric pottery wheel.

One sits and forms the pot, the other two spin it for him.

I, the helper, don't help them do any of this. Zero. They do not need me to. That took a while to understand. All I needed to do was build a workshop for them to work in, search for designs that people will buy, and communicate with customers so they can sell what they make.

As "helpers" in the world, we often do TOO MUCH.

When we operate out of guilt and arrogance it is disrespectful to the men and women we work with. We can come in thinking far too little about the capacity of the people surrounding us. The vast majority of people don't need to be carried down the road, but they do need a road and it does need to be somewhat passable.

For those of us that can build roads and remove some of the larger boulders, we do well to stick to that.

~ 19 ~

ENTER FOREIGN HELPERS

"AND AS YOU WISH THAT OTHERS WOULD DO TO YOU,
DO SO TO THEM."
LUKE 6:31

I have found faithful the decision-making grid "do unto others as you would have it done unto you." So if I imagine the narrative of international disaster relief flipped and my American community being the ones in need it looks like this:

What if our small town in South Georgia was hit by a Natural Disaster? It destroyed all industries, schools, churches, and the businesses where my husband and I both worked. It took out the internet, phone service, electricity, and clean water supply. It tore away all the normal ways we cared for ourselves and our kids.

What if the story of our demise reached the shores of Japan and out of great compassion, the people of Japan came to see for themselves our desperate situations.

What if they soon began leading teams of people here to help us. Unfortunately, we could not understand their language, nor could they understand us. There was a longing to communicate, but it was no use trying. We settled for the imperfect grasp of one another's meaning behind actions and expressions. They came with food, generators, water, and tents. We were grateful.

What if they stayed for a month or two and kept the warm meals coming and set up emergency water supplies and temporary housing for our kids, we'd be ok with that. Especially since we no longer had jobs and couldn't afford diapers for the baby or soap to wash their clothes. It would be a relief to see our kids cared for again after we had lost so much.

But what if they brought more and more people with this foreign language to our neighborhoods. And they came with their cameras and wanted their pictures taken with us in our lowered state. Me in my crappy clothes, my hair desperately needing to be colored, and my shoes full of holes. No make-up. House still in disrepair. And these visitors walked freely onto our property, bearing expensive gifts to our children when we were in need of concrete blocks and tin for the roof.

Just think about it. In this scenario, our kids might begin to think that these foreigners are the ones that truly love them. I mean, they are the ones bringing new shoes and soccer balls. While we, the parents are struggling to keep the roof from leaking. We're in rags, they're in Land Rovers. We're losing dignity. And our kids are losing respect for us.

How much would I love that?

I think I would not be so thrilled with their help.

I think I would say if you want to help, build real businesses, register them, pay taxes to our local government here and employ local people. Bring people in that will listen to us and potentially invest in our business ideas. Help us grow our capacity. This way we can get back on our feet and become independent of you.

Remind us that we are strong and capable and that we have much to bring to the world.

I think I would want that.

~ 20 ~

THE BEST GARBAGE

ONE WOMAN'S TRASH...

There they sat, surrounded by their bounty: plastic spoons, some broken plates, tiny packets of shampoo, and a hot sauce bottle with fragments of usable juice. These kids, maybe 5, 7, and 8 years old took turns turning the bottle up into their mouths, happy to get the drops. There was an old computer keyboard and some broken figurines. Three barefoot kids in the shade, going through the goods they'd just found while combing through the dump.

And this is what they do. Everyday. Scavenge among the garbage of Gonaives on the edge of the beautiful Jubilee.

One day I was out at the salt flats on my little yellow motorcycle. I used to ride out there for the sheer joy of it on trails that wind around the salt ponds. It was like riding through hard-packed sand dunes. It felt good to smell the wind off the ocean and to have the warm sun on my face. Especially after a stressful afternoon of get-

118

ting yelled at by the jewelry makers or breaking up fights between them that I had most likely caused by my terrible language skills.

I took off past the garbage and rode around the ponds and out to the sea. Sometimes I would just park there a minute and feel. Quickly I was surrounded by kids, we chatted a while then I rode back. On that particular day as I was headed back, I saw a familiar truck.

Our truck.

I saw our truck, and in the driver's seat, the young man that did maintenance on the vehicles and helped with projects. I saw him coming through the community and past the school and over the first piles of garbage until he came to a stop.

Children and old people ran toward him as if he were the second coming.

I watched in horror as our garbage... my garbage from my bedroom and our kitchen and my daughter's room was dumped into the community where I worked. And I realized they could see everything about me, about us. They could see the expensive bottles of shampoo and empty chip bags, salt and barbeque still clinging to the foil. They could read in our trash the stories of our days.

And I watched as people tore open the bags and clambered for the contents.

I was speechless.

I wanted to scream and I wanted to hide. Or better yet cease to exist altogether. The kid that had hitched a ride back from the sea with me was watching the scene from the seat behind me, leaning on my back. She said, yeah, everyone gets excited when the white truck shows up with garbage from your house. It's the best garbage.

It's the best garbage.

I have nothing against using recycled materials. In fact, it is what I do. And I think that it is great for children to be smart and help their families. But, honestly, picking through the dump can be a desperate attempt at life, if it is all there is. It is dangerous to pick through garbage that is set on fire with each truck that dumps it. These kids are barefoot and the fumes are toxic.

Funny how you can ignore a thing like where does your garbage go when someone else hauls it off. Funny how you can stand so self-righteously and call out disdain for the city trucks that come roaring past day in and day out to bring the cities garbage to the backyard of the community you love. Funny. Until you realize not only are you part of the problem but also that the stuff you throw away is considered the good stuff.

The Best Garbage.

~ 21 ~

BASKET PRICES HAVE GONE UP!

"PAYING GOOD WAGES IS NOT CHARITY AT ALL-IT
IS THE BEST KIND OF BUSINESS."
HENRY FORD

I had the honor of sitting with the two talented artisans who oversee one of the basket guilds. They are brother and sister and have been making baskets for over 20 years. I wish everyone could sit and look into their faces and know them a little.

The basketmakers.

They called me into a meeting and asked if we might be able to raise the price a bit on a few of the baskets, citing the cost of materials had gone up and gotten more difficult to find in the aftermath of a destructive hurricane.

I said I would look and see how it would affect our customers and get back to them.

I did.

And I began to feel this tension.

If we paid them more, it would cause our customers' price to go up too. How would that work? Most people that shop with us are stretching their dollars as it is.

These talented artisans were very happy to have orders coming in. They would continue to work at whatever price we said we could pay. It is the nature of living at the "bottom of the pyramid". It is why companies take their work "offshore". Labor is plentiful and it is as cheap as you want it to be.

It is as cheap as you want it to be.

Are you weeping yet?

Because I really am?

It's no wonder ancient texts warn us, the rich, about taking advantage of the poor. Because we can. And God, the father of all of us, feels pretty strongly about that kind of behavior.

I sat with them and decidedly told them:
If we aren't walking justly, we need to close our doors. Period.

So I asked that they be open with me about the time it takes to make them and what is a good and just price. They talked and I took notes.

I went back into our inventory system and I looked. I saw how these changes would affect our customers. These people chose us when there were cheaper brands of baskets out there.

And I worried a little, will we keep selling them? The last thing I wanted to do was to bring fewer orders to this group of skilled makers.

I decided to do it. I decided to raise the price so we could pay the artisans more. So we could pay them what they believed was a fair wage. I believed it too.

A few days later we made this announcement to our customers: **We've raised our prices on our baskets!**

The bargain for our customers was that when they bought one at the new price, they knew that they were paying a just price. A fair wage. And I was betting that is actually what our customers wanted from us more than anything else. And I was right.

~ 22 ~

RICH IN FAITH AND CORN STEW

"LISTEN.ISN'T IT TRUE THAT GOD
PICKED THE POOR IN THE WORLD TO BE RICH IN FAITH
AND THEIR KIDS INHERIT ALL THE TREASURES."
JAMES 2:5-6

Once again, I was slain.

I started my day battling a dark cloud that was attempting to set up residence in my mind. It happens. Sometimes it is a little gray poof of a cloud and other days it is so vast and dark I can barely see a pinprick of light. Do I struggle with depression? Does anyone not? I have come to think of it as a rhythm. Most days are up and then a few days go down.

This day was down.

I climbed on my sturdy yellow motorcycle and drove through town, crying out for a way of escape from my own head. Wishing

I could leave it on a street corner somewhere and get on with my day. But no. There was no escape. My head came with me.

I made my way down to the seaside community I had grown to love: Home to most of the moms and dads working their trades to become successful artisans. This small neighborhood where many houses are built with broken blocks and discarded sheets of tin. Where I inevitably learn best.

I needed to take spools of twine to Anite, the cotton cord flower maker. She had moved up from sewing patches together to make flowers. I rolled up and parked outside her tiny rock-built home. And soon I ended up sitting on a solid concrete block on the floor in the house of Anite. Though I only came to bring her supplies, she welcomed me in to visit.

She invited me to taste the yummy dish that I had watched her and her children working on the day before when they were pounding the corn with a big wooden mortar and pestle. It looked like something ancient and brilliant.

Apparently, it takes about 24 hours to make this dish.

Did you catch that?

They had been working on this one dish for 24 hours. Starting with a mortar and pestle pounding the corn. Not sure what happens next. But there is no fridge. There is no food processor. There is no electricity or even a table.

But now it was ready and there was an air of celebration in the anticipation of filling bellies with this dish.

I don't know how long it had been since this family had all had sufficient calories for their tiny bodies in a day. "Not enough calories" is the primary cause of illness in this neighborhood.

She tells me that I have arrived just in time. She and her four kids, one neighbor child, and one more teenage girl welcomed me with huge smiles. She dished up a generous helping of the delicious corn-bean stew onto tin plates for everyone present. She handed me one of the few spoons and watched my face. They all did. "Li Goo!' I cried. "It is good." It really was.

She then dished up a bowl for the teenage boy that followed me in.

Then:
She tried to give me a dish to bring home for my daughter, too.
She tried to give me a dish to bring home for my daughter, too.
She tried to give me a dish to bring home for my daughter, too.

Generosity.

Out of poverty.

I was slain.

That afternoon I got back on my yellow motorcycle and made my way through the city to home.

There was no more gray sky.

The dark cloud that had settled in my mind was no match for what I had just experienced.

Many boxes of free rice had shown up at this house over the many months Anite and her kids lived there. The kind that charitable organizations lovingly pack and ship to needy people. And they were always grateful to receive it. So grateful.

But this day they weren't the needy people.

They were the rich.

~ 23 ~

AROUND THE EDGES

"IT IS IRONIC THAT WE MUST GO TO THE EDGE TO FIND THE CENTER,
BUT THAT IS WHAT PROPHETS, HERMITS
AND MYSTICS INVARIABLY DO."
RICHARD ROHR

Some days overflow with hope. These days explode with signs of ruins rebuilt and a noisy cacophony of chains falling off our shackled feet. God is everywhere and in every face.

Other days Grim Perspective comes to hang out for a while.

And all we see are:

- Children still naked, playing in the dirt
- People still begging, "give me one dollar"
- Despair and hunger, terrible accidents, and children still contracting TB and malaria.

All over the world, some days are just harder.

I walked through beautiful Jubilee and struggled to see the beauty.

I was feeling like a huge failure, and that turned everything to gray.

I glanced toward the once hopeful Garden Project and all I could see was dirt. Lots and lots of brown dirt with garbage blown in and accumulating in piles. The gate was wide open, offering free grazing for every lucky pig and goat. I was bummed entirely.

How hard we all had worked to get stuff to grow here. How many plants had been planted, how much dirt had we brought in? How much water had been hauled in five-gallon buckets from the pump to this dirt?

And then I heard a tiny whisper of a thought: *look closer.*

Around the edges.

And so I did. And I realized there were actual trees. 10 - 12 foot tall trees. Two of them. They are there growing just fine. They weren't there before and now they are.

Around the edges.

Small shoots of Cactus, planted months ago in hope that a natural barrier would be established to protect young plants from scavenging goats, are taking root and spreading up and down.

Around the edges.

An Oleander with a few pink flowers was there. Growing, because I guess the goats somehow knew they were poisonous. Such smart goats.

They are there.

Around the edges.

Some days are almost overwhelming and it seems like life is so ruthless with us. Can we all not just BE for a few minutes without the depths of human pain, without being aware of our personal desperate failures. On those days would someone please remind me to stop and look closer, around the edges.

Because around the edges, I can see that Christella, who makes the Christella Hope necklace, is almost finished building her own sturdy block house with the money she earns by making jewelry. Around the edges, I see that another family has built a private toilet in their small yard to protect their daughters from using a more public place. Around the edges, I see that the school added a library when kind friends came and delivered books and computers and all the things it takes to make that happen.

How easy it is to miss the important stuff happening on the edges. Oh God, please fix my broken eyes!

~ 24 ~

THE NAKED KID WITH CLOTHES

"A PICTURE IS NOT ALWAYS WORTH A THOUSAND WORDS. SOME-
TIMES YOU NEED MORE INFORMATION."

KB

I sat with a friend in her house in Jubilee. We were perched on her bed talking when her 4-year-old came in from school. He was adorable in his neat little shorts, checked shirt, and shiny black shoes. He carefully undressed and folded his uniform, laid it on the bed where we sat and ran outside to play.

San (without) clothes.

Clothes are truly unnecessary in the yard where he plays with the other kids who have also made it home from school and carefully left their uniforms folded on their parents' beds.

After a while, he ran back inside and started trying to get into one of the suitcases that served as a chest of drawers. Apparently playing in the yard had evolved into "going down the street". I watched this little guy attempt to wrestle a pair of pants from the suitcase. Once his momma realized what he was up to she told him to stop. I asked her if he wanted to pull the pants out to wear. She said, "Oh yes, he loves to wear clothes. He often sneaks in and puts on clothes when I am not watching." We laughed.

I asked her why she didn't let him. She said it's because washing them is so much work!

So there we have it: Some children are naked not because of a lack of clothes, but because of a lack of washing machines! Because in big families the act of washing clothes by hand each week is an all-day event. Especially when you are drawing the water up from a neighbor's well or carrying it from a nearby stream. This is every woman's Saturday.

I remember taking a picture of this particular kid one day. Because back then I did that when the kids begged me to. I took it from the angle above his head as he looked up at the camera. He is a beautiful child so the photo is adorable. In the photo, you couldn't see that he had on bright white little boy underwear. He looked like he was clothes-less. When I ran across the image later I realized how sometimes an image is NOT worth a thousand words.

Looking at the photo one could have created an entire narrative about this "poor child". You would never know that he just carefully folded his bright clean uniform and laid it on his mother's bed. You would never know that it was really too hot out to wear clothes anyway if you didn't have to. You would never know that he came from a two-parent home with their own water source and strongly built house. You'd not know that he is one of the smartest kids in his class and that he is in church every time the doors are open.

You'd never know that he has a very full case of clothes just steps away that his mama simply doesn't want to have to add to the mountainous load of clothes to wash come Saturday morning.

Is the neighborhood "poor" by anyone's description? Definitely. But is he? I would say not. I would say he is a happy kid in a family working hard to make a good life for themselves. I would say there's more to the story. His story.

~ 25 ~

NOT BACKING DOWN

"PROCLAIM THE TRUTH AND DO NOT BE SILENT THROUGH FEAR."
ST. CATHERINE OF SIENA

I sat there in the tiny room we call our warehouse and I looked at the bins of jewelry made from recycled bits of broken glass and journals covered in burlap coffee sacks and the handbags, hand-sewn, imperfectly, hanging from the corners of the shelves. There were not quite symmetrical baskets stacked high in the corner and the uneven braided rugs folded over the work table.

It is small.
Such a small showing of the work we give our lives to. I thought to myself.

I heard a familiar voice agree:
Yes, it is so small.

But this voice wasn't saying it is beautiful small, no, it was saying it is pathetic small.

It was accusing me. It ridiculed me:
So very, very small, it said again.

It was the craggily voice of the Discourager that added:

So why? Why do you do it? It is so small. It is doomed to failure and it is way too hard. Why keep going? You and I both know you can't actually do this. You don't know what you are doing. You're clueless, really. You're not gifted in business

This voice ripped at me in my most vulnerable places. He seemed to know them well.

Not only is it small and impossible, but you're also all alone foolish little you.

Next, he tried posing as my Voice of Reason:

Come on. Smarten up. It's ok, you tried, you gave it your best shot. You can console yourself with that thought.

Shifting into that slimy, "I am your friend" angle.

And for a few dark moments, I wanted to run and hide. The poison seeped into my mind. I was weak. I was tired and probably dehydrated as I so often was. My weakened mind darted around, seeking a way out. A way to stop fighting and surrender to discouragement.

How about death, he generously offered. *You could make it look like an accident. I can help.*

At this, something snapped inside. Now he had gone too far. Showed his true hand.

I shook my head as if to get free. Then a flicker, a tiny bead of light.

A wanting of the light even.

And that is all it took.

I reached out to my partner in life, my husband, in the room next door and told him the battle going on in my head. It took that flicker of light to give me the breath to do that. To bring my dark thoughts into the light.

And together we began to do the only thing we knew to do.

We began to give thanks. First without feeling, without conviction. With willpower alone.

We began this battle with the most feeble of strength.

Thank you for our good health, and again for tables to work on, and again for a good supply of boxes, and again and again. Thank you for our kids. Thank you for the calories we had today.

Speaking these words out loud knowing that each utterance of gratitude was a sling of the proverbial blade in this fierce battle taking place in the unseen places of our minds and perhaps the cosmos.

Soon the tiny speck of light took form and our energy grew.

It was as if we were caught up in some medieval brawl. We picked up a larger sword and a huge shield landed in our hands.

And we remembered.

We know these weapons. Yes, we do. They are more real than the air we take into our lungs, more real than everything we see with our eyes.

In those few moments, this goofy couple in their mid 50's were transformed into dread warriors. Mr. "O your work is so small you should die" is going to be sorry he ever whispered that crap in our house!

We thanked ourselves into drunken joy. We began to battle for the lives of ones we love and ones that matter so very much to heaven! Small ones, hidden ones, families we know, and families to come.

And then it came, the battle cry!

WE WILL NOT BACK DOWN. WE WILL NOT STOP.

We will not faint before the fear of failure, fear of not being enough, fear of being all alone in it.

I do believe that there is a force that would very much like it all to stop.

Every dream to see the world a better place. Every heart set toward "on earth as it is in heaven." Everyone that has given their lives to play their part in this great restoration symphony.

There is a dark force who would like very much for those ones to give up. To step down.

But we mustn't. All it takes for evil to take this planet, more greed, more children sacrificed on the altar of disparate systems of brokenness, more empty bellies, ignorance, and hate, is for little folks like us, ones who know better, to do nothing. To back down, afraid.

This warehouse may be small, so very small. But it represents the lives of real men and women and real hope. It represents real food, real beauty coming out of really beautiful people.

This matters enough to say to fear, *I see you but you're not the biggest player on the field.*

We are not backing down.

IV. Build up the Leaders

~ 26 ~

FROM TRIAGE TO BUILDING A COMPANY

"IF YOU WANT TO WALK FAST, WALK ALONE. BUT IF YOU WANT TO
WALK FAR, WALK TOGETHER."
AFRICAN PROVERB

The concept of company building was foreign to me in the beginning. In the early years, I treated this work as the scene of a very big, very bad accident. We were doing triage. I was constantly trying to evaluate who in the community was most needy and then racked my brain to figure out what work they could do so that they would not die of hunger or lose their kids to orphanages.

It was a big leap for me to begin thinking about hiring qualified people with experience in business, not just people that were the most in need if we were going to make 2nd Story Goods sustainable.

I was resistant to it even. I questioned if I was selling out if I hired local people who finished school and had gone to college. Was that even right? We were focused on bringing jobs only where signs of poverty were clear and visible.

The truth was and still is that people who graduate from college are just as desperate to find jobs as anyone else in a country with a 70% unemployment rate.

And as I said before, I didn't even know that I wanted to build a company. Initially, I thought I'd help get these groups of Makers up and going then I could leave them with it. They'd each be their own small business and grow it themselves and I would back out of the picture.

But when I shared that idea with the leaders of the groups, they said, *No. You can't do that. We have to walk together.*

Just because they had become Makers of jewelry, didn't mean they were now ready to do business in an international market. How silly that I didn't realize that from the start. How arrogant of me to think this was all there was to it.

But I knew nothing about building a company. I knew a lot about building a family. And I **loved** doing that. That was my dream job. How much harder could this be than that? I mean I don't actually have to give birth here, or nurse anyone for 10 months! I did graduate from University, but not in Business. In Communication. (I should have paid closer attention in my French Classes!)

I needed information quickly. No time to leave Haiti and go back to school and get an MBA. So I did what anyone living in a foreign land needing education quickly would do: I Googled it.

And I began to listen to podcasts about building a company while pedaling my bike in the early mornings around the city. That body of knowledge quickly turned toward raising leaders for the next generation. And I remember thinking, this **is** like raising a family!

I wrote in my journal that day:
I want to build a Company. That is what I want to do. Not just create jobs, but build a lovely, thriving company.

This is a very different thing than Triage. This is not emergency relief. This is building something for the future. Something that will outlast me.

It took a good bit of humbling to realize that a company consists of people with all kinds of skill sets. And if we were going to become something sustainable, and I was not going to kill myself working 100 hours a week in the process, I needed to be open to hiring more people in the city.

Enter Ariel Dorval.

Initially, he was introduced to us as a young man who spoke English and had a degree in Accounting. Ariel is to this day one of the people that I respect most on this planet: small of stature yet a giant among men, always dressed in a way that made you know he paid attention to details. We'd tease him and call him "fresh". His smile was captivating and his words certain. At the time I thought, *At last, someone I can hand off the work of the day-to-day cash flow.* That took a huge load off of me. I was no longer carrying around a purse filled with money. Ariel managed it. He was our new bookkeeper. And after months of working side by side, I realized he was more than that. He was a true leader.

I loved watching the way the artisans trusted him. And believe me, it was not easy to earn their trust. He would sit and listen, really listen. Then he spoke, slowly and with wisdom. So he quickly was promoted to head of HR, because that was what he was.

A few years later we were working hard to complete our 2nd Story Clothes collection for Spring when I realized we had two serious problems:

#1 The sewing group was arriving to work later and later each day, first 30 minutes, now 1 hour and 30 minutes!

#2 People were using their phones to watch videos while at work and that signaled a lack of respect for the manager.

Early Friday morning I gathered the Sewing Manager, Phillipe, and Ariel for a quick conversation told them my concerns, and asked for their opinions. I made a few suggestions, *like I do*, then turned it over to Ariel to fix it. Also, *like I do.*

I saw them gather the sewing team to an outside table to talk. I was concerned they would be too hard on everyone, and that the makers in the sewing group would feel unheard or unappreciated.

But an hour later the sewing group came out all smiles and said, *That was a great meeting!*

What?

I went directly to the office to find Ariel.

What happened? I asked.

He was all smiles and said,

I really like this sewing group. No. I love them. They have such great attitudes and they were so glad we called them out on these two things. They really want to make it better.

What did you do? I asked.

Ariel started the meeting reminding the team of the pressure Phillipe carries as a manager every day to continue to get it right and to bring our sewing standards up to the place we all want them to be. Because he carries the reputation of the company on his shoulders, he explained to the group, we must all respect his job as a leader in the group!

He told me they didn't even have to make a rule about the phones. He just asked questions and the team suggested the rules! As far as coming in late, I had suggested we send everyone home for the day. But Ariel told the sewing manager:

Tell them that as a result of not starting on time, we won't work today. They made that decision by not arriving on time. They are the ones in power. Their choices lead.

Ariel led the Makers to see that they have the power and responsibility for their lives, their well-being, and the future of their families. He led through love and because of that, justice came through. This is the picture of leadership.

This is what it takes to build a company.

~ 27 ~

EVALUATION: THE BRAVE QUESTION

"HOW WOULD YOU DO IT DIFFERENTLY IF YOU WERE ME?"

ANDY STANLEY

I am soberly aware of the critical role I play as leader of 2nd Story Goods. This tribe of people trust me, not to be perfect but to give it my best. To be my best.

Someone once asked me,
What is the most difficult part of working in a developing nation?

I answered honestly,

It's the same thing that is hard about working in the developed world.

The woman in the mirror. Me. I am the hardest part.

This question came about the same time we changed our mind-set from doing poverty triage to building a real company. And I knew that the success or failure of this company, to a large percent, depended on my willingness to deal with me. I was going to have to go deep and do the interior work I had avoided for years.

So I said to God:

Now you are going to have to get serious. You and I both know we have been way too gentle on the darkened stuff in my soul. You've allowed me to keep my dimly lit rooms where fear and ego live so comfortably as room-mates. And they have caused the whole house to wobble. It is time. You have my complete permission to go after that mess and clean me out.

By shadowy stuff, I am talking about emotional and relational detours I jumped on when threatened. These were shadowy, twisted paths I'd run down to hide, protecting myself from unpleasant conversations and scary confrontations. The path was dotted with familiar signposts, supporting my choice to avoid real people with real opinions. And I would use a religious spirit to drive me. This was helpful because, with that, my ever huge, ever fragile ego stayed intact.

Just me and Jesus. He is all I need. I don't have to deal with the rest of you people. And I don't have to look honestly at what is going on inside of me that makes you feel so scary. Just me and Jesus.

O my.
One can not build a team this way.

I searched for help and found, "The Art of Inviting Feedback", an Andy Stanley Leadership Podcast episode. This is where I first heard the brave question:

How would you do it differently if you were me?

I thought, are you kidding me? If I ask that question of my colleagues they will crush me. They will point out all of my faults, my inconsistencies, my failures and I will lose all credibility as a leader. This will take me directly into the unpleasant conversations and confrontations I am trying to avoid!

The podcast explains that Leaders are generally surrounded by people who have opinions about how they can do their jobs better. That is good information. The problem is that if we don't ask for it, we don't get it. And most of us are too insecure to ask. We are afraid. We don't realize that avoiding the question is not negating the answer. The podcast explained:

When a leader announces that they are going to tell everyone about their personal weakness, no one is reaching for a pen to write it down. They already know.

How would you do it differently if you were me?

I had to soak on the idea of asking the brave question for a while. I needed to be ready to ask. I needed to be ready to listen and bravely hear the response.

So I prayed for humility and grace. And for an escape from my old twisty ways.

And a few weeks later I arrived at the place where it mattered more to hear the responses and get better at leading than it did to continue to prop up my own fragile ego.

So I set the appointments with my top three leaders who were most affected by my leadership tactics. I gave them the evaluation forms that included The Brave Question. And then I gave them a few days to ponder their responses.

And I prayed some more.

Eventually, the day of reckoning came, and scared and shaky, I met with each of them all in one day.

How would you do it differently if you were me?

#1 Complaint: I needed to remember to stay in my lane. I was in the habit of stepping out of my lane, and by doing so, I was undermining the authority of the managers. That looked like me going and sitting with the Jewelry Makers and chatting about how they were doing with different designs, or how they felt about the pay on this piece or that one. A big no-no. That was a conversation for the manager, not me.

#2 Complaint: Delegate. I needed to improve. Give others responsibility and then trust them to handle it. Don't hover. Don't manipulate. Let it succeed or fail on others' shoulders.

#3 Complaint: Lead Spiritually. This one surprised me. I never wanted to force any spiritual system on anyone working in this company, and yet, they told me in these meetings, that it was my spiritual leadership that attracted them to the company, and I had sort of left that part of me behind. They wanted me to bring that back: Go ahead and pray with the different teams and share what God was doing in my life.

Mostly they confirmed to me some things I knew I was doing wrong and some things I never would have seen without their help.

The big takeaway of this exercise was likely that they understood that I truly valued their opinions and that they had real leadership clout in the company. You keep good people when they know that. You build a sustainable company with people when they know that.

And I discovered that their insight was both freeing and valuable to me! It began the construction of a new road. Instead of looking for a detour around or a place to hide from unpleasant conversations, The Brave Question made me want to walk through them. I began wanting to know what they knew. Wanting to change with their help.

What I'd thought of as unpleasant became a place of learning.

I'm not naive enough to believe it will be this way each time I ask, but I dare to ask it anyway.

How would you do it differently if you were me?

~ 28 ~

OPEN HANDS AND THE PAPER
MACHE VASE

"PLEASE, TELL ME WHAT YOU SEE. CAN YOU DESCRIBE IT?
WHAT ELSE? TELL ME MORE." KB

As we developed our leadership team, I realized that we needed to have more Big Awkward Conversations. We were dancing around issues that I believed stemmed from the mere fact that we were coming from different cultures and life experiences. I was nervous, certain I was part of the problem but had no idea how to fix it. So I called us together. A group of six.

We were

- Three women, Three men
- Four people raised in Haiti, Two people raised in the United States
- One Baby Boomer, Five Millennials
- Three married people, Three single people
- Two of us with kids, Four without

And we talked through hard things.

Open hands

I heard author Bob Goff share this great trick. According to his research, there is a direct correlation between the posture of our hands and the posture of our heart.

By simply making the choice to flip open our hands, our brain gets the signal to open up and listen, be vulnerable and receive what the person is giving. Our hands' posture convinces our minds that we'll be ok.

In his book, *Love Does*, Goff writes:
"When people get angry or defensive they tend to make mistakes. But nobody can be defensive with their palms up. Palms up means you have nothing to hide and nothing to gain or lose. Palms up means you are **strong enough to be vulnerable**, even with your enemies. Even when you have been tremendously wronged."

This simple gesture communicates that there is nothing to protect or defend here and nothing to hide. *I am here to be transparent and to receive what is brought to me. I am big and I get to decide what to do with this information.*

This little trick helped much.

Because if we don't have the difficult awkward talks, we can't lead well, we don't grow closer to the important people in our lives and we don't get stronger as humans in our evolving process. We can't build great companies. And we get stuck.

The day of our Great Awkward Conversation we sat around the round table and these issues came up:

- How we feel when teams of visitors come to visit and try to teach us how to brush our teeth or sew simple bags. Things we do quite well, thank you. There was great humiliation in allowing high school and college kids posing as teachers to come in and "teach" those much older and wiser. Why was I as the leader allowing this to happen?

- The shame we feel when the news covers our street demonstrations that turn violent and how people get only a fraction of the story. When even foreigners living here tell stories and post pictures that make it look like the whole country is in flames, when it is only a few isolated incidents and over quickly.

- And we talked about money and the use of it. How it feels when our paychecks are $50 a week and we see Americans spend $50 on a single meal for 2 at the local hotel.

We talked long and hard. We heard each other. We leaned in and we listened. And I kept my palms turned up resting quietly there on my thighs under the table. Yes, I did.

And then I had this GORGEOUS revelation.

We had this paper machè vase on our round table. I bought it years ago in Jacmel and filled it with colorful silk flowers. It was one constant thing in my dusty imperfect living space that sparked joy.

The vase had vertical stripes of color and designs. And while we were having the Awkward Conversation, I was distracted by the vase. It had something to say too.

I realized that what I saw of the design from my seat at the table was different from what the young man two seats to my left saw from his spot. Which was different from what the young mother one seat to my right saw as well.

A BIG AHA!

I could have described the vase in detail. I would have talked about the lovely shade of orange with the red tiny flowers. So matter of fact. But the truth is that only I could see it - me and maybe the person directly to my right, but certainly not the person across the table. They could not imagine what I was talking about. While they would have talked long and hard about the blue stripe with the green leaf design, and I would be like... What's wrong with you? It is orange. Are you blind?

So the vase woke me. And I realized that What I see, I see simply because of where I am seated. And the Wise Me accepts that my reality is not everyone's. The Wise Me says to the person across the table:

Please, tell me what you see. Can you describe it?

What else? Tell me more.

The Wise Me knows I have many more blind spots than I have clear vision spots. The Wise Me is grateful to find people that sit across the table and know stuff I don't know. The Wise Me is respectful and curious and delighted to learn.

The Wise Me is always mindful of my upturned palms
and this colorful vase.

If we are going to turn this huge HELPING revolution from hurting to doing some good, we must actually sit differently in our chairs. We must imagine that colorful vase between us and the person or community we have come to engage.

We must walk humbly. Come in asking for help. Come in as a learner. Come in honoring our blindness and the vision of others. We'd be so wise to start with:

What do you see that I don't see?

And, what would you like to tell me about that?

~ 29 ~

SOON YOU WILL BE DEAD

"REMEMBERING THAT I'LL BE DEAD SOON IS THE MOST IMPORTANT TOOL I'VE EVER ENCOUNTERED TO HELP ME MAKE THE BIG CHOICES IN LIFE."
STEVE JOBS

I'm not sure where I picked up this idea of the 10-minute essay. But I've been using it for 20 years. It is simple, yet profound. Every single time.

I started it when our kids were home. I'd give them a quote to write at the top of the paper, usually something from Ghandi:

Earth provides enough to satisfy every man's needs, but not every man's greed.

Or Nelson Mandela:

Education is the most powerful weapon which you can use to change the world.

Jesus even:

Blessed are you who are poor, for yours is the kingdom of God. Blessed are you who are hungry now, for you will be filled. Blessed are you who weep now, for you will laugh.

The oldest kids would groan a little, then put their pens to motion and write for a solid ten minutes. Anyone can write for 10 minutes. That is the premise. I still have the sheets of paper where Rebecca, the youngest at three years old, would sit at the table too and "write" her essay. Then when we'd take turns going around the table to read aloud she would proudly hold her paper full of circles and lines and tell us her thoughts. The girl always had thoughts.

I use this exercise with groups visiting Haiti, with our 2nd Story Goods staff, and even at the start of every board of directors meeting. I found out that 65-year-olds complain just as much as 13-year-olds! But they do it, and it is ALWAYS amazing.

In a recent staff meeting, I played a video of Steve Jobs' famous 2005 commencement speech at Stanford University.

We watched the video, stopping to translate along the way, and then we passed out pens and paper and set the timer for 10 minutes. The simple instructions were to write about what most stood out from his speech. And then I sat at the table and watched as everyone went deep in thought. I could see the subtle shift in thinking. To me, this is the big stuff. I live for these moments.

As I began to write I realized the part of his speech that most spoke to me was "remember you'll soon be dead."

Jobs said:
Remembering that I'll be dead soon is the most important tool I've ever encountered to help me make the big choices in life. Because almost everything — all external expectations, all pride, all fear of embarrassment or failure — these things just fall away in the face of death, leaving only what is truly important. Remembering that you are going to die is the best way I

know to avoid the trap of thinking you have something to lose. You are already naked. There is no reason not to follow your heart.

There is no reason not to follow your heart!

Nothing clarifies life like a death sentence. And we all have one. None of us make it out of here alive. So I decided to get more intentional. What do I want to give the world before I exit?

This is the thought that went through my head that day.

Remember you'll be dead soon.

I wrote it down and put it on my desk. Something shifted inside me.

If I'll be dead soon then it's time to get my eyes off me and how I am doing. It's time to stop caring if anyone likes me, and concentrate my fury of energy on growing up the young leaders around me.

My inner mantra became, you don't have to like me, but if you get on board this bus that is 2nd Story Goods, then, You Will Be Great! I will be clear with you and honest and will love you enough to fire you if need be. But if you stay here, you will become great at who and what you want to be. We won't have figureheads that take home a paycheck but haven't a clue how to do the work. We'll have confident women and men that know stuff.

I promised one of my favorite employees that after three months if he simply could not do the work that the job required, I would let him go and find the person who could. Yes. I said it. He just looked at me with wide eyes and shook his head with a slight grin. *Thank you, Mk. That is the best thing you could say to me.*

See. When we work in developing spaces one of the biggest mistakes we make is a basic lack of respect. We think that people cannot really do the work that is needed. So we water it down, lower our expectations, and treat adults like children. And you know what? They know it.

The worst thing I can do as a leader is put someone in a high-level position but go behind his back and do his work. Fix his work. Make excuses for him. That is so humiliating.

Instead, I promised the young man that if he still had the position in six months it would be because he was working his butt off, doing the work no one else could do, and feeling exhausted at the end of the day.

I'll be dead soon but they will carry on.

~ 30 ~

NICOLE AND THE REPOSSESSED
SEWING MACHINE

"YOUR WORD IS YOUR HONOR. IF YOU SAY YOU'RE GOING TO DO
SOMETHING, THEN YOU NEED TO DO IT."
ANONYMOUS

Nicole arrived at the school, mud splashed across her flip flops and up to the hem of her blue skirt. On her back, with his arms wrapped tightly around her neck, was the beautiful boy in his pressed school uniform, crisp white socks and shiny black shoes.

It had rained the night before, turning the salt flat into a mud-flat. Not to be deterred, Nicole, weighing in at just 88 lbs. loaded her handsome grandson on her back and sacrificed her own clean state to get him to school on time and immaculate. One of the smaller of the sacrifices she has made, no doubt.

Nicole is a tiny woman, feisty and fierce. She is a survivor of floods, earthquakes, and systemic poverty. And she is raising her grandson now, on her own. Raising him to be smart and kind and resourceful in every way.

For work she takes in clothes that need to be altered and mends them by hand.

She approached me one day after visiting us in the sewing workshop and asked if she could have a sewing machine. She said she would pay for it over time if we would buy it for her now. After consulting with Mafie, the faithful and wise leader among us, and Ariel, our keeper of the books, we decided that would be a great investment. Clearly, Nicole was a woman we all wanted to see win.

We decided to buy a brand new treadle machine, powered by a foot pedal. These machines are great where there is no electricity. They always work! We walked together the six blocks into the city center to the local shop that had one for sale. Nicole looked it over and agreed it was perfect for her. Ecstatic, we hired a driver to carry it to her house and we began the walk back.

Mafie and I sat with her and wrote up a payment schedule. I hung back in the conversation, not wanting to screw it up with my lack of knowing.

Life ensued and she made the payments as planned. The first two. Then they stopped. Every now and then Mafie would tell me that she sent someone to collect them and they always came back empty-handed. I would have forgotten about it entirely if it weren't for Mafie's diligence and then, the conversation with Lala.

Remember Lala? Lala the fierce leader of the Jubilee School? She knew all about Nicole and her new sewing machine. I had bragged about the business arrangement that would enable Nicole to make more money, and the fact that we weren't doing "charity" but instead making a reasonable investment of funds.

Lala: How is it going with Nicole and the sewing machine?
Me: Great, I guess. (sheepishly... I mean define "great")

Lala: Is she making the payments on time?
Me: Well, no. She stopped making the payments after the second month.

Lala: What are you going to do about that? What was your agreement?
Me: Well in the contract it says we will repossess it if she doesn't make the payments.

Lala: So when are you going to do that?
Me: Lala! I can't go over there to that tiny concrete house in the middle of Jubilee and drag a sewing machine away from a tiny widow raising her tiny beautiful grandson. Are you freaking kidding me?

Lala: Oh, so you want the community to know that you are a liar.
Me: WHAT?

Lala: The entire community knows about your arrangement with Nicole. So if you don't do what you said you are going to do everyone will know it. They will not respect you or your words from here out.

I need to say here that EVERYONE needs a friend like Lala in their life. I love her and she loves me and she has a strong NO BULLSH*T gene that can both bless and beat you up in the best sort of way.

I could just imagine backing up to Nicole's tiny blockhouse and forcefully dragging said sewing machine out the door and lifting it into the back of our big white truck. I imagined hundreds of people from the community gathering around, yelling horrible things at me, threatening to throw rocks, telling me to leave and never come back.

See, at that time I was still peeling away the outer layers of my white saviorism. I was still giving pity rather than respect. I was treating people lacking resources as children or somehow lacking in intelligence. Nothing could be farther from the truth.

Generally, people lacking resources have become extremely intelligent in order to survive. Nicole was no exception.

But dang, Lala. Dang.

I consulted Mafie once again. Always Mafie.

What do you think Mafie? Do you think she is having trouble making the payments? Could we offer her a new smaller payment schedule? Can we go back and again try to collect even a small amount? Give me something to go back to Lala with to prove that I am not the worm it looks like I am!

Mafie looked me square in the face and said,
Mk, I think perhaps she doesn't want to keep the machine because if she did, she would make the payments. She has plenty of work and could make the payments if she wanted to.

Mic drop.

Nicole was, to me, one of the friendliest people in Jubilee. She would go out of her way to walk by and say hello. She would always ask about my kids and check to see how we were doing. Always.

But ever since we were in this lender/debtor agreement, she would turn the other way when she saw me coming. She never dropped in to just say hi. I hated that. I missed her.

So the horrible terrible awful day came and I had to go do it. I had to go and actually repossess a sewing machine from a respected woman in the community. A person trying hard to raise her grandson. It was a step in the path of respect over pity and honoring my word over doing what felt easier.

So I climbed up in the truck, went and picked up Beaver and our dear friend Josh, and asked them to go do it for me. I did. I really did.

I jumped out at the workshop and left them to go the rest of the way to her house without me. Yes, I did.

When Beaver and Josh arrived at her house, she smiled and said, *Here it is*, as she pointed to the machine. They lifted it into the back of the truck, hugged her neck, and drove to the workshop where I was pretending to work as wave after wave of anxiety rolled through my chest. When I saw them come back so quickly, I thought something must have gone bad wrong.

Nope, they said. She was fine. No problems at all. No crowds gathered around, no bad words said. No one even looked up from their porches.

The very next day, Nicole was back to stopping me on the road to ask about my family and share a hug. So there.

~ 31 ~

LEVERAGE THAT WHITE PRIVILEGE

"WHITE PRIVILEGE IS AN ABSENCE OF THE CONSEQUENCES OF
RACISM. AN ABSENCE OF STRUCTURAL DISCRIMINATION, AN AB-
SENCE OF YOUR RACE BEING VIEWED AS A PROBLEM FIRST AND FORE-
MOST."
RENI EDDO-LODGE

I sat in the lobby of one of the nicest hotels in Haiti.

The Marriott had recently opened and it was gorgeous by any standards. The designers were brilliant in their use of local art, Caribbean sunlight and open space. Huge pieces of Metal sculpture were hung artfully from the 30-foot ceilings. The entire place was spacious and filled with light. There was a family of life-size paper maché goats that greeted visitors at the reception desk. The dining room featured a collection of 12-foot square paintings highlighting traditional art that mingled edgy with ancient. The tables were generous with space and elegant in design and comfort.

And I was there waiting for an appointment with the newly appointed General Manager. I asked myself, How did this happen?

I came to Haiti to live and work with the poorest of the poor. To spend my days walking through salt flats and the garbage dump. I came to learn from and create jobs for people that will likely never step foot in a place like this. Had I gotten lost? Had I betrayed my true calling, sitting on that comfy stool?

I shook my head. I was pretty uncomfortable in this dust-free place of elegance dressed in my less than lovely linen pants that I proudly purchased in the street market for less than a dollar. And while I waited I began to wonder if the once white sleeveless shirt I threw on early this morning in my dimly lit bedroom, before I began the three-hour drive to Port Au Prince, might have a small hole in the back? And my shoes! I was suddenly conscious of my ever dusty, inelegant, Chaco sandals.

Yes, always the Chacos. You see the truth is that even if I left my house driving a car or truck, I sometimes ended up walking. It happened when cars died mid-trip, or mudslides blocked the road. It happened regularly when upset people created manifestations, blocking the road for car travel, making it impossible to get to the airport by car. On those days we had to get out, grab bags and start walking in hopes of finding a Moto taxi that would take us the rest of the way. I had experienced all of the above, so that I only wore shoes that I could walk in for miles, just in case. Hence, the dusty Chaco sandals.

As I sat there in that elegant space, I wondered if the nicely dressed, clean people, who clearly had access to hot showers in their rooms upstairs, could smell the dirt on my sandals and the dust that clings to my wild locked hair.

In this clean, artful space I couldn't help but wonder if the leadership team of our growing company from Gonaives and Jubilee, people I love dearly and do life with daily, would ever see or experience this side of their own country.

I was acutely aware that a percentage of the reason I was there was due to my own lack of melanin. I am considered white in the socially constructed system of race. And that has many ramifications. One of which is that even slightly dusty and in worn-out, ugly sandals, I was welcome in this place. The doors swung open and I was greeted warmly by the men that guard them. No questions asked.

Since moving to Haiti I had become acutely aware of both white privilege and white liability. I learned to navigate both.

The truth was that most gates opened for me when I drove up, simply because of the shade of my outermost layer. It was a sign and wonder.

The fact that some people were compelled to yell bad words at me as I pedaled past on my bike simply because of the shade of my outermost layer, was also a sign and wonder.

We learned to navigate.

So there I sat.

I just happened to have met the General Manager as she was part of a group that came through our store and workshop in Gonaives a few days earlier. She looked around, saw our sewing group, and asked if we could make napkins. Yes, I said we absolutely can make napkins. So here I was, a few days later, in Port Au Prince with fabric samples waiting to meet with Ellen, the General Manager of the nicest Hotel I have ever been in in my life.

She was a delightful woman from Holland. We became fast friends. I have this great love and respect for Dutch women. They are the opposite of me: A Southern woman. They speak directly, unapologetically and without guilt or shame. I now have four women in my life who are Dutch. I treasure their friendship and I am hoping their brave way of being in the world will transform me.

As I asked Ellen her story and how she ended up with this position, she shared her history in the hotel business. It was long and successful. And when she was approached with the offer to come to Port Au Prince, to manage this place, she knew she couldn't say no. She came because she too wanted to be part of the solution. She wanted to lend her skill set to help create a successful business here that would employ hundreds of people and promote locally sourced products.

She and I were the same.

Here's a little dark secret from the world of "charity work". It is easy to think highly of oneself when one spends their days among the poorest of the poor, working in the dumps and with people living in rusty tin homes. One can develop a sense of arrogance thinking, *I am the "true" missionary. I am the one really making a difference in the world.* And it is easy to cast suspicious eyes at those who wear nice shoes and walk on carpeted hallways and take meetings on marble floors. But that's just silly. And I am ashamed of that shadow within me. I have repented.

It is painful when you realize that in a country where the majority of people have skin that is mostly rich in melanin, I, the minority by far, still carry the privilege. In most circles. If a person with dark skin and deemed inappropriately dressed, tries to enter the same hotel, they can be asked for ID, for their bag or simply asked to leave. It is this way. It is not a good way. It will not always be this way. But it is now.

So while I took up a seat meant for customers I made myself a promise, not to change my skin color but to use it - to leverage it for all it is worth for the dream of jobs and dignity.

Yes ma'am we can make 400 napkins. Yes, we can.

~ 32 ~

PA FOT MWEN - IT'S NOT MY FAULT

"THE PRICE OF GREATNESS IS RESPONSIBILITY"

WINSTON CHURCHILL

It is easy to take responsibility for mistakes if your life experiences have rewarded you for doing so. If your parents, teachers, workspace has applauded honesty and humility and owning your mistakes.

It is **HEROIC** to take responsibility for mistakes when your life experiences are not that. There are cultures where you are literally kicked out of the tribe for mistakes. In those families and workspaces, there is seldom forgiveness and redemption. It is scary to admit a mistake. In that climate, we engineer spectacular means to hide, disguise and confuse any perceived wrongdoing. It is the way of survival.

The big problem with this is that healthy societies, families, and companies can not be built on shame and hiding. But only on truth and vulnerability. Businesses grow, relationships thrive, government offices work only when it is safe to come forward with a mistake. As leaders, if we are really smart, we will highlight and applaud that courage. This helps dismantle the system of shame.

Pa fot mwen (not my fault) is the phrase used to hide mistakes. It is the epitome of an unhealthy culture.

In 2nd Story Goods leadership team meetings, we have talked about how the idea of *pa fot mwen* fights against us. Because the very definition of leadership is one that takes responsibility. So when we use the phrase, Not My Fault, we are shouting *I am not a leader! Don't look to me to do great and important things.*

So to encourage and reward the admitting of mistakes we decided to celebrate them.

A few years back someone caught a big mistake in our Inventory Management System. Clearly, the warehouse manager had tried to fix some duplicate entries, and in doing so deleted very important data. A big, but perfect mistake.

The reason I call this the Perfect Mistake is because:

#1 He made the mistake while trying to "Make it Better", which is one of our seven core values. No one told him to do that work, he was taking it on himself to try to make something in the company better. A great mistake!

#2 As soon as his manager explained that in fact, the system doesn't work that way, he owned it! He said out loud, *I made a mistake. I'm sorry for that. What can I do to fix it!*

In Haiti **pa fot mwen/not my fault** is heard more often than you might imagine. Once we sat and recounted the many lines we've heard. Hilarious things like, *I didn't hit you, my hand did!* Or *I didn't drop the glass, it fell from my hand.* More stories were shared and we laughed big.

I should add here that in Haiti the term Pa Fot Mwen can also be translated, "I didn't mean to do it". There are gradients to the use of the phrase. Kreyol is a high context language. So this phrase can be misunderstood, especially by non native speakers.

And still, when I heard this young man say, *I made a mistake,* that was all I needed to hear. I saw a leader.

Today, even the smallest admission of *I made a mistake* causes us to get ridiculously happy (maybe even jump up and down with clapping). Because another great truth I've learned is this.

What you give attention to, you get more of.

And if we congratulate people for coming forward with mistakes, it will happen more often.

Also, as the point person in our company, our leadership team has full responsibility to call me out on my mistakes and they do! *Mk, you must stay in your lane. Mk, you are being grumpy, you need to go take a rest. Mk, you don't understand the culture behind this.* And it is always done with honor and kindness. But believe me, they do it! And each time it makes me so glad to be a part of this type of culture.

We can build on this.

~ 33 ~

JUSTICE

"THE ARC OF THE MORAL UNIVERSE IS LONG,
BUT IT BENDS TOWARD JUSTICE."
--MARTIN LUTHER KING,JR.

A few years ago I was pretty much minding my own business when I had this conversation with The Voice:

We need to talk about Justice.

I responded, *Sorry, I really don't understand much about Justice.*

And The Voice said *I realize that, but I do. How about this, I'll talk, you listen.*

At that point, I realized that I was afraid of the word and the very concept of Justice. I had a feeling that it was about angry fists raised in the air, burning tires, and smashing storefronts. I did not understand.

But then The Voice explained it this way:

Justice is simply reaping what you sow. True justice is the capacity to act and receive the consequences of that action. With nothing standing in your way.

I'd never heard it that way before.

When understood this way, Justice is actually one of the most basic components of what it means to be human. It is a central characteristic of being a free and intelligent agent.

With Justice, there is a direct correlation between what I do and what happens next.

The person who exercises self-control and doesn't eat all the corn, but saves some back to plant, reaps the reward. That person has a whole new crop of corn in the fall. There is a direct line of cause and effect.

Injustice occurs when we plant and sow and work hard to save back seed to plant, but then some bully comes along and steals those seeds, or reaps the rewards of our choice to do all that work. That is injustice.

Haiti, as we know it today, was founded in an unjust system.

Remember Christopher Columbus? Our hero?

He didn't step foot in the USA we know today. But he did land on the island he named Hispaniola. Today it is Haiti, which was colonized by the French on the west and by Spain on the east: The Dominican Republic.

He landed in Haiti in December of 1492. There are tales of how horribly he and his men treated the native Taino and Arawak people. As explorers and colonizers were accustomed to doing, they took control by force and enslaved the local people. Many died because of diseases the Europeans introduced into the environment.

Having pretty much wiped out the Native population, the colonists began to look elsewhere for laborers. All eyes turned to Africa. The people were strong and able to work hard in the harsh sun. The French who controlled this Caribbean shore needed people like that to grow and harvest the cotton, sugar, coffee and indigo that was making them ultra-wealthy.

So instead of offering living wages to a community of people already there and opening the borders to immigration of their colonized lands, they found people that traded in human beings and sold them for profit. The Colonizers bought these kidnapped ones and set out to strip them of their unique identity and basic humanity.

There are no words to describe this period of time when men and women and children were treated by other men and women and children as sub-human. The depth of depravity in a person's soul that could look on another human this way, is unfathomable. It is part of humanity's most shameful history.

The nation of Haiti became known as the richest of all the French Colonies. It was the fanciest place to live. There were huge homes and elaborate theaters. The island of Hispaniola was the place to be for wealthy Europeans.

But the people who were doing the hard work to make it so were not involved in the fruit of their labor. They weren't gaining wealth or negotiating contracts with buyers. They weren't creating education systems for their children or passing laws to govern their communities.

Others were.

The clear connection between sowing and reaping was broken.

I think this is what the Voice was trying to teach me in the most simple terms.

In 1804 the strong people that had been horrifically enslaved won their independence from the broken-minded enslavers. And now the men and women of African descent were free to rule the land. What had become Haiti, was now theirs.

But there had been 300 years of building and strengthening an ugly, sub-human system of injustice. 300 years of power plays, of treating humans like animals used to pull carts and work until they dropped. 300 years of bullying and scheming and stepping on the necks of the population.

The role of "Boss" was that of a tyrant, not a leader striving to create systems where everyone could thrive. "Bosses" created systems to keep the working people as weak as possible. They had to keep a shroud of powerlessness over the enslaved ones in order to keep their global economic game in play. Everything was broken in terms of leadership.

True leaders make people see their own goodness and power. True leaders share responsibility for the tribe. True leaders create more leaders. And all of this works well where Justice flows. Where we truly reap what we sow. But when you have a culture and a big economic force that sits on the back of injustice to carry it, then everything is crippled.

And therefore everything was broken in terms of feeling pride and personal connection to the work of your hands.

300 years.

Think about how deeply the colonizer's enslaver way of life had been ingrained into society and culture. There were no memories of freedom. There were no memories or models of good leadership that propelled systems and communities forward, making life better for all. There were no models of education systems that ensured that the youth would be strong leaders ready to take the place of the generations before them.

The restoration of Justice has been in effect for just 200 years. It is a long sure process. And it is critical that we understand the importance of restoring that connection. The connection between reaping and sowing. This basic Human tenant.

Because the truth is our poorly thought out charity can do exactly the same thing as slavery.

Charity can do exactly the same thing as slavery.

It can break that connection. When we bring in tons of stuff and give it to the people who can show us they are the poorest of the poor, what are we doing but establishing a connection between poverty and reaping?

We in essence tell people the best thing you have going for you is your poverty. *We will reward you for that.*

That is messed up.

And horrifying when you realize that after many years you can train an entire proud culture to become beggars. You can strip them of dignity yet again.

I remember clearly one day a lady came to see me. We had bought some of her woven pieces in the past. She did a good job and we always called her when we needed more. So one day she comes to me. And she lead the conversation by telling me that she has so many problems and she needs work. She told me how her husband has been sick, how her kids need new shoes, how the rent was due, and on and on. She was pitching me from her place of need, her position of lack. She was wagering that I would "give" her work because of her problems. In essence, I had trained people to believe that in my early days. I used to like being the savior in these moments. I used to think that was the loving role to play. But not anymore.

So when she finished stating her case I picked up one of the braided pieces that she made.

Do you know why we purchase these from you? She glanced up from her downcast eyes.

We buy them from you because look, see the way you put the colors together? You have an eye for that. You are brilliant with colors (She almost smiled.) *And feel this, see how well the stitches hold together? You take your time and you do it well. Your pieces never fall apart.* (Definitely got a raised chin and a sparkle in the eye at this remark.)

I went on:

I agree, your problems are serious, and I am so sorry that this is a tough time for you and your family. We'll pray into this. But the truth is we buy these from you because you are good at making them. Period. Not because you have problems. But because you have talent.

> *I am here to give you a place to show the world what you have,*
>   *not what you don't have.*

I thought to myself that I will never tell another living soul that I said that thing. It sounded so mean! But I so wanted to get the point across to her clearly: problems are not your asset, your brilliant work is.

Justice.

YOU are in control of your own destiny. You have this job because you are good at it! You respect it! You are a helpful part of a team! You reap what you sow. Your actions have consequences. You have power.

Both slavery and charity can remove that sense of personal power and responsibility. But Justice restores power and responsibility, and building a company is a great place to practice.

~ 34 ~

TOP 5 HABITS TO AVOID AS A LEADER

"IF YOUR ACTIONS CREATE A LEGACY THAT INSPIRES OTHERS TO DREAM MORE, LEARN MORE, DO MORE AND BECOME MORE, THEN YOU ARE AN EXCELLENT LEADER."
--DOLLY PARTON

#1

Avoid thinking that you are the smartest person at the table. What a big freedom to remember that we brought these people onto our team because they are good at what they do and they can see things I cannot possibly see. I try to avoid thinking that I am the smartest person at the table and celebrate the truth that I was smart enough to hire smart people!

#2

Avoid perpetuating a chaotic environment. Personally, I kind of enjoy a level of chaos and spontaneity. But I realize that for others this creates mountains of stress. I need to maintain a healthy level of "let's try this in the moment" but at the same time recognize that we have systems in place and people feel secure when we follow the systems. I try to avoid creating unnecessary stress!

#3

Avoid focusing on faults. When I am lazy I make judgments on people. I focus on what they are doing wrong rather than on how we can adjust the system to make it easier for them to do the right thing. For example: when a manager was consistently late getting to work, instead of creating a mind of judgment toward him, we created a sign-in sheet and let everyone know, they would be paid in full for the days they arrived on time! Then I could see their work objectively. You don't need to judge, because the system is keeping them accountable. Then you can focus on what is right, not on their faults, and freely give praise for work well done.

#4

Avoid comparing yourself to other leaders in the same space. This never goes well. But it is a constant challenge! I am ridiculously insecure some days and when I see others come out with products that I wish we had made I feel like such a loser boss! I have figured out what helps get my head straight: I choose to cheerlead and promote. I choose to send an email and say, *Girl you are killing it with that new collection.* Because the truth is there is room for all of us in the market. And comparing myself to others poisons my flow. Cheering others on and truly celebrating their good work fills me with the good stuff!

#5

Avoid straying out of your lane. As founder-director, this has been one of the most difficult disciplines, because we founders used to do it all. But now we have this beautiful company. We have systems. We have org charts. We have job descriptions. I cannot tell you the number of times our staff has called me out on this "straying" I do. *Mk, this isn't your lane,* Mafie will ever so gently tell me when I am entering a quality control conversation that she is managing just fine on her own. When I avoid straying and let others do their jobs, they learn and grow and we create stability in the company.

~ 35 ~

PEOPLE LIKE ME GET BETTER
WITH AGE

"GETTING OLD IS A FASCINATING THING. THE OLDER YOU GET,
THE OLDER YOU WANT TO GET." KEITH RICHARDS

I sat with two of my co-workers and we rewrote job descriptions. His and mine and hers. I was letting go of things. We were moving them over to his column.

She was taking control. She was managing me. Giving me boundaries and writing work to do. Banishing me out of workspace flow for hours at a time. Giving me space to go deep.

And he asked me:
How does it feel, Mk? How does it feel to be giving up some of your jobs? Are you afraid?

I told him:

*Last night I overheard a meeting going on between three of our leaders.
I didn't initiate the meeting. I wasn't invited to the meeting. I only knew
about the meeting because it took place using the internet of our home.*

And it thrilled me! I was giddy with delight!

I think one of the keys to growing our little company has been
my willingness to continually slide work over to others that I no
longer need to be doing and trust them to make mistakes and grow
and in the long run, do it better than me!

I kept the things I do best. And I'm still working hard to make
that list shrink. My most important work is that of continually calling the young ones up into new areas of expertise and expanding
their skills.

I am not afraid of being replaced. I am working toward it.

I have other things after this. As I told him...
My true skill sets only get better with age.
My best paintings have yet to be painted.
My best writing has yet to be written.
You see, people like me, we get better with age.

V. How it Changed Me

~ 36 ~

DISMANTLE

I have learned that it is wise to stop clinging to the rickety and familiar if those things are found unstable and untrue.

I have learned the Art of Dismantle.

But I hate it. I hate taking things apart. Especially things that look fine just as they are. Perhaps less than perfect, but good enough.

Years ago, our oldest son Brandon and I turned a pole barn at the farm into an adorable Gift/Art/Junk Boutique using old painted doors and peeling shutters. In ONE day!

It looked adorable.

A strong wind could have blown it over. But it was sure cute. Then Beaver came home from a business trip and said, *no, honey, just no.* He knew stuff we didn't know about engineering and support walls and such. And when the day soon came to take it apart to build something more permanent, I whined about it. I was proud of my made-in-a-day adorable shop.

But in order to have a real shop, I had to let it go. I had to dismantle the cute flimsy thing.

I've learned this is true with many things in life. I still dislike it.

It is hard to dismantle things because, generally speaking, someone has buy-in to what already exists. And generally speaking, they don't want to knock it down. If the current state of things has value to us we will fight hard to keep it as is.

The Market Place Gonaives building was such a great and enormously painful lesson to us in the very literal Art of Dismantling. And by "us" I mean Beaver and I and all of the people who invested their hard-earned money toward it. Let me explain.

In 2014, my husband and I dreamed of buying a huge old warehouse in the heart of Gonaives. Our vision was to renovate it to become a hub for economic and cultural development. It would be home to 2nd Story Goods and it would be a place that would call Entrepreneurs and Investors to the city. It would bring in tons of jobs, help stabilize the city and enable families to stay together and thrive right here in Haiti so that fathers and mothers would not be tempted to fly to Brazil to find work or put their kids in orphanages to secure daily food. It was and is a beautiful dream.

I distinctly remember the morning after the evening when we'd sat with friends around the long table at the Big House, and wrote it all out on a big piece of butcher paper. We used colorful pens and everyone added their pieces of the vision. It was wild and at one point included tree houses, drum circles, and communal showers for weary travelers!

That next morning I woke and made my way to the shared kitchen to find the coffee percolation already underway. We brewed a huge pot each morning, sometimes two. And whoever woke first was in charge of getting it started. I waited a few minutes, washing up dishes until the perking was done. I poured the scorching hot liquid and grabbed my journal and headed to my perch on the swing in the backyard.

There I sat in the dim light and thought about the dream. We had written it down. It was now a real thing. We were going to go after it. But it was going to cost money. Serious money. Like a million dollars of money.

I remember sitting there knowing full well we had about 300 dollars to our name. Not a million.

That morning, in that swing, I felt like Heaven told me one very important thing.

I see you, I know you don't have a million dollars.

Strangely I had opened the scriptures to the passage where Mary and Martha are heading to the cave where the soldiers laid Jesus' body after his lynching. Martha was freaking out along the way, fearful that they would get there and not be able to move the giant boulder the soldiers had rolled in front of it.

As I read, I imagined the scene. Martha, longing to get to the friend she loved and care for his body with the honor and respect he deserved, yet scared all along the way. But when they rounded the last bend, they saw the cave and the stone was already pushed aside.

That's when I heard the message.

That million dollars? I know you can't move that stone. That is not yours to move. You just keep walking. That is your job. I got the stone.

After much consulting of people smarter than us and many months of drawing plans and wrestling with budgets, miracle of miracles the funds began to come in. People, friends of friends, literally came to visit us in Gonaives, walked with us through the salt flats and saw our tiny attempts at job creation and then said to us, *You should ask us for money.*

But why? I asked. *Why ask you?*

We had no idea who these people were.

Because we are on the Board of Directors for a large Foundation. We give money to work like this. And you see that guy? He is the Chairman of the Board.

Oh, I thought. *What is a Foundation?*

Yes, that is how naive and ignorant we began this work.

On the advice of people we trusted deeply, we hired a well-known and respected local engineer to oversee the entire renovation project. I'd love to describe this process here, but honestly, I don't yet think I can. Let's just say that three years in and many hundreds of thousands of dollars later, the building was renovated and it looked good.

It was beautiful by all standards.

It was probably twice as strong as any building in the city.

It was a cool place. An impressive place. A lovely place. A source of pride for us. We were a few weeks from being ready to move in. We only needed a few more cosmetic adjustments and to have the Seismic Testing done by an outside engineering firm, certified and internationally accredited to do such studies. No problem, our engineer said, *We will pass with no problem.*

Except, we didn't.

Our beautiful pride and joy of a building did not pass the seismic testing. Not at all. It was not earthquake safe.

This matters because Haiti is bordered on the north and south by two major fault lines. It is a place on the earth where pressure is released every so many years as plates shift. Kind of like the fact that Haiti is also in the path of hurricanes that spin off the northwest coast of Africa.

It doesn't have to be disastrous. As long as buildings are built to stand when they shake, it is not disastrous. We have the technology to do that. The world has had the technology for many many years. The 2007 Peru earthquake, which measured 8.0, killed just over 500 people. The earthquake that hit Haiti measured 7.8 on the same scale in 2010 killed close to 250,000 people.

A month later after more visits by the engineers, we found out just how bad it was.

We had to take down every wall: The ones we had just built and even the exterior walls that had been a part of the building since its inception.

Every wall.

Every block.

The sound of the sledgehammers working day and night rang throughout the property. Big trucks came in and carted the rubble away and were used to fill in the low places on the grounds of Jubilee.

Fitting.

But we had no choice. We could not un-know what we knew from the report. It was a huge decision, but not a hard one. One quick Google search revealed the images of the damage done by the earthquake that hit Port Au Prince in 2010 and there was no argument. Many said the loss of over 200,000 lives was not a natural disaster, but an engineering one.

We could easily see how that could have been the case had we not dismantled the MPG (Market Place Gonaives) building. Because in the dismantling process we saw entire block walls that had zero iron rebar in them.

Zero.

Seeing it with my own eyes made us want to throw up. How? How could someone build so carelessly and how could we have not noticed it happening under our noses.

We had to face our Board of Directors with the full extent of the report. We were ashamed and heartbroken by what felt like a horrible betrayal of the engineer, who we had thought of as a friend.

Covered in this great sadness and shame we flew to Atlanta for our Board meeting. I'll never forget the dinner where we gathered casually after being picked up from the airport. It's become a habit for a few of us who can meet for Mexican Food that first night to spend time together as friends before the heavy board meetings of the next day begin.

I was nervous and so so sad. Beaver and I walked slow and heavy, not knowing how angry these friends would be with us. Not knowing if they would even want to see us before the meeting. We were exhausted from the stress of the previous weeks in Haiti and anxious at what was in store in Atlanta. We were a mess. About as broken as we've ever felt.

You see our board is heavily involved and committed to the work. They walk their talk. They give sacrificially. And with grateful hearts, in those first few hours of arriving in the US, they made it clear to us, *We are here for you. We care about you first. We'll figure out the next steps for the building, but are you guys ok?*

I just wept. Such grace.

I felt like this entire project had been the climb of a lifetime, up the steepest and most trying terrain. And then days before move-in time, we made it to the top, legs trembling, only to straighten up and see that now we faced an impossible rock face. I had nothing left for this last piece. Nothing.

But fortunately, we did not climb alone. Back in Haiti our Haitian friends took us by the hands, literally took our hands, made a big circle and started to pray, in the way that people who have seen floods and earthquakes and injustices unspeakable know how to pray. My faith was so puny in light of what these ones carry. They said to us, *We have faith for this part. We'll pull you and Beaver the rest of the way. Our faith.*

And they did.

When the dismantling process was over it was a see-through building. Only the center posts, floors, and roof remained. It was eerily beautiful as the sunset behind it. We sat on our porch and watched it descend. You're not supposed to be able to see the sunset through a concrete building. But we could. It still makes me a little sick to my stomach to think about it.

I do not dismantle well.

By late 2020, we had completed the refit. The entire building has been rebuilt to the engineering firm's stringent seismic safety plans. I shake my head in wonder at how the funds came in and continue to come in just as needed. We never have more than we need each week, but we always have enough. We are scheduled to open soon. It is miraculous to me.

~ 37 ~

THE CAMPUS OF MY LIFE

"IN ALL AFFAIRS IT'S A HEALTHY THING NOW AND THEN TO HANG A
QUESTION MARK ON THE THINGS YOU
HAVE LONG TAKEN FOR GRANTED."
BERTRAND RUSSELL

If I think of my life as a campus of beliefs, there are more than a couple of buildings that have not passed seismic testing. I still have a couple of fine-looking structures that are untrue and unstable and need to be dismantled.

To name a few:

There is an US and a THEM.

This is such a lovely little building on my campus of belief. Because as humans we are first tribal if we are nothing else. The oldest part of our brain knows that our survival depends on being part of a tribe. So the US and THEM structure is difficult to destroy. It is also a sturdy part of our ego. As long as we are US, we are better in so many ways than THEM.

I notice the cracks in this building when I see things in me that I have always said are a part of THEM. I hate it when that happens. For example, I judge the woman who becomes paranoid when her husband engages me in conversation at an event. *She is so immature and unspiritual.* I think to myself. *She is being ridiculous and silly.* She is one of THEM.

And then the moment some young woman skooches her tight little body up close to my man for a personal conversation, I go ballistic. *I'll cut you,* I think to myself and almost say out loud. Boom! There it is. I am one of THEM.

Jesus tried hard to get the message across: There is no US and THEM. Which was difficult in his day because the narrative of the Jewish people and probably all the people groups of that day was built on the premise that we are US and we are clearly God's favorite people. And you? You are not.

Jesus kept striking heavy-fisted blows on the walls of this building in scenes like the Good Muslim. I mean the Good Samaritan. And the "not going to throw stones" story, when all of US stood in a circle around the woman with rocks in our hands and he said, **Not me. Not joining you guys. If you don't have any sin, please feel free to start the rock-throwing. But understand I am not a part of this circle of US.**

To be fair, Jesus expected quite a grand leap from these men. He was asking them to find themselves in her. To dismantle, if you will, that sturdy, safe wall that says:

WE are a part of this group of righteous men and we have nothing in common with you poor unrighteous woman, caught in bed with a man, not your husband. We are other than you. In fact, you are truly below US.

Jesus was asking them to take the sledgehammer to the wall of separation that kept peering eyes from the windows of their own souls. Admitting that they are not different, but the same is the walk of true humility. Jesus modeled it and searched for it in the community.

He utterly wrecked the US and THEM structure, and somehow I still manage to patch up and rebuild this one on the campus of my life about three times a week.

The year 2020 has gotten us into one of the most polarized seasons of our history. We're in a season of picking our camp and staying with it. Finding our "US" and pointing our fingers at the "THEM".

We are rigidly divided between the Right and Left, the Blue and Red states, the Progressives and Fundamentalist religious sectors, Black Lives Matter and All Lives Matter, Sexual Identity spaces and even sports teams!

Without the walls, without the US and THEM shack, we easily see our similarities, the fears and beauty we share. It takes great, extraordinary courage to dismantle this shack. Because without it we're vulnerable, unprotected by the crowd, but we're free.

The next building:
Nothing bad can happen to you when you are good with God.

How did we ever build this shack? The facade of it is flashy if not a bit ridiculous. It reminds me of the way we often decorate for parties in where our walls are crumbling, We go out and borrow shiny curtain sets and string them across the walls to give an air of respect to the space. We create an appearance that says *we're all fancy here, everything is good with us.* But we never don't know we're sitting in a building that could be blown over in a strong wind.

The only way you can keep building one of these **Nothing Bad can happen to you when you are good with God** shacks on your campus is to keep judging and putting distance between you and the ones who have suffered.

And then when your day of suffering comes, you have to do an even more flimsy and tacky addition. An Addendum to the "no bad thing can happen to me" that says something like:

- I am such a badass in God that the devil is really scared of me so he tried to take me out, or
- God let that happen to me so I can teach other people from my experience. I am in commando training. I am that good, or
- This was bad but actually really good, I am sick in bed because Jesus is trying to teach me to rest.

Each add-on is worse than the last.

Don't get me wrong, I am all for taking charge of the narrative of our lives. Tell it how we see it. We get to do that. But, it is important to accept that bad things do happen to all of us. It doesn't mean God is not happy with us or that we did anything wrong or right. It just happened.

But where do we go from there?

I've watched the most beautiful people I know walk the shadowy hallways of cancer, lost babies and suffered the untimely death of spouses and parents. Each time I found myself popping the nails out of the boards of this flimsy structure. It just could not stand up to real life. That building is gone. The beautiful people and their lives laced with grace, remain.

The last building:
Everything works out well in the end.

This building on my campus I built as my safe house. I needed it because my faith was weak. Now I wonder how I possibly kept this shaky shack held upright.

It doesn't always end well. Sometimes it just ends. I used to need a lovely ribbon wrapping up the narrative in order to prove God is in control.

People, God is not in control. Rapes, Wars, Greed, Child Abuse. That is not the work of God. That is the work of us, the dark fearful side of us. We are in control, and we get to yield our control to Heaven and follow the ways of love. Or Not. It is our choice.

And because of that and natural disasters and cancer, sometimes things don't end well. They just end. But this is the thing I know. And you might not actually believe me on this.

When things don't end well, God is with us still. And THAT is enough.

I had a friend once ask, *Where is God when the mother in Syria is trying to shield her babies from the bombs falling on her town? Where is God when justice is denied in the court and the young innocent black kids are sentenced to 20 years for a crime they didn't commit? Where is God when the father doesn't come home from Iraq, or the corner store?*

Where do you think?

He is there. Right smack dab in the middle of that moment. He is there. Huddled around that momma in Syria shielding her babies. He is there in her, being God to her babies too. He walks, arm slung around the young man cuffed and terrified as he makes his way from the courtroom. He is always found in those places.

This I know.

It doesn't always work out well in the end. It sometimes just ends and for those broken enough to let the light in, we see that God is there still.

So I have dismantled that building that kept threatening to slide down the embankment where it was perched. I used to like to sit on its porch, trying to look casual as I used my arms to hold the teetering baluster in place. I'd make up pithy sayings to call out to the suffering ones passing by unless of course, they were too distraught, then I'd just slip inside and cover my ears to drown out their cries.

The building is no longer there. It has been successfully dismantled. It is just an empty lot of wildflowers growing over the things that have simply ended, watered with the tears shed in that place.

~ 38 ~

THIS AND THAT

"THERE IS NO US AND THEM.
THERE IS SIMPLY A LOT OF THIS AND THAT INSIDE US ALL."

KB

Currently, I am in a season of trying to figure out my relationship with the sacred text known as the Bible. We are trying to make up because in essence, we've had a big fight. And now we sit together politely speaking only on points where we can agree.

It is a brave gesture on my part. These writings and all the many thousand coats of men talking about them helped to erect the "us and them" idea of humanity.

That building on the Campus of my life, I am working to dismantle.

Some of the sacred writings enforce it. And it has become a habit we believers have brought into this century. A habit I hope we break out of soon. Like a toddler that sucks his fingers. It's not a thing to carry into adolescence.

I was recently reading about Peter, the good friend of Jesus, proclaiming so boldly that he would never deny Christ.

If everyone else falls away and denies you, I won't! I will die with you if I must, but I would never deny you. I am one of the faithful. I am the US, the true believers.

He proclaimed like only we religious zealots can!

And we all know the story. Give him 24 hours of life-threatening pressure and our dear brother Peter caved.

But to be fair, wouldn't we all like to think that? That we would be firmly planted in the camp of the "Us", The Faithful? Never to stumble into the land of the "Them", the Deny-ers.

Take for example, "Us" the Pro-Lifers. We love unborn people, and value humanity and would never hurt another human being. As opposed to THEM, the Pro-choicers. Those people we imagine don't have proper respect for life or care about people in general.

Months ago on my bike ride down a quiet road on the edge of Gonaives, I passed a man sitting on the side of the road. He appeared to be bone thin. His torn jacket was pulled up over his head, I imagined, to give himself the tiniest scrap of shade. And I wondered, had he sat down to die?

It was mid-morning. Already 90 degrees. Did I mention how impossibly thin he was?

And I passed him by. I saw him clearly.

And I had the thought, "he is probably going to die there".

Just like that.

I wondered if he was mentally ill or just... done. I wondered if anyone was looking for him. I wondered how old he was and was he thirsty or hungry. I wondered if I stopped to talk to him if he would surprise me and reach out and grab me with the strength of blind rage, hunger or desperation.

And I kept pedaling. Right past him.

And I wondered,
How could I?

How I could pedal right past him, A fellow human? And how could I be more concerned about my own well-being/schedule/ comfort and not stop? How I could simply not want to get in- volved?

I have rallied at the pro-life events. I have taken into my home pregnant women in need of shelter. I have counseled young women as they find out the shocking news that they are carrying a new life inside of their own bodies knowing full well that was not at all what they had planned for their life. I have sat with the mother that had to make the excruciating decision to terminate the life of her much wanted unborn child, due to severe health issues, so she could be alive to care for her baby at home.

And I have pedaled right past dying people.

I beg to think there is no "us and them".

Instead, there might be "this and that" inside of us all.

I do believe in setting good policies in our nations that protect us from injustices. Don't get me wrong. I think we are designed for this.

My point is:

We are broken. I am broken. I am surrounded by people that are about five days away from death if their caloric intake gets threatened. I am doing what I can to edge us all back from that cliff. But at the same time, I can callously pedal past a dying man.

I can't imagine harming a baby in its womb time or any time. I also can't imagine pedaling past a dying man and not stopping to help.

But I did. I do.

I believe we are a broken people on a journey toward getting whole. We have a ways to go. I have a ways to go.

~ 39 ~

WE WERE ROBBED

"WHAT SEEMS TO BE CLEAR IS THAT WE HUMANS ARE AN ACCUMU-
LATION OF OUR TRAUMATIC EXPERIENCES, THAT EACH TRAUMA
CONTRIBUTES TO OUR BIOLOGY, AND THAT THIS BIOLOGY DETER-
MINES, TO SOME EXTENT, HOW WE RESPOND TO FURTHER TRAU-
MATIC EVENTS AS THEY EMERGE IN OUR LIVES."

SHAILI JAIN

We experienced a home invasion in April 2016. And it changed me.

I am tempted to say "our" home invasion instead of "a" home invasion. It seems weird that I would claim ownership to a "home invasion" as if it is a collection of words and actions and emotions thrown in a box stored out in the shed or something. *Honey, hand me down our Home Invasion box,* she calls from her desk as she writes.

I am still to this day, jumpy when there is a knock on the door and when I hear doors open if I don't know who is coming in. I ALWAYS lock the door when I am inside alone, even if only for a few minutes. I am hyper-vigilant about the people who have access to my space and I have developed a weird need to have all the keys with me at all times.

Three years after the event I had my first appointment with a licensed therapist in the USA. I arrived and got through the initial overview of our story and life style, when the therapist asked me if I could be suffering some PTSD from the home Invasion event she and I had lightly discussed

No, I said, point-blank. *We were surrounded by lots of people praying for us. I'm sure that is not causing me any problems now. I think my current stress has to do with the state of things in Haiti today.*

At this point in Gonaives, we had been under Country Lockdown for months. (Peyi Lok) Gas shortages, cash shortages, businesses closing, our 2nd Story Goods sales plummeting, staff scared for their lives at times, angry crowds, sometimes violent masses of people marching up and down our street. Surely that was the real issue.

She nodded her head knowingly, not wanting to disrespect my grand hypothesis, I am sure. Then asked, *Mind if I poke around in there a bit? Ask a question to two?*

She asked one question.

I was calm and as unemotional as can be. And then she asked:

What was the hardest part of that night?

And instantly a huge wave of fear and a solid wall of tears exploded from somewhere deep inside me.

What was the hardest part of that night?

When they took our son from the room and we could no longer see him. That was it. There is no terror for a mom like the kind that happens when angry armed men take your child out of your line of vision and you have no idea what they are going to do to him.

Four men climbed the wall and broke into our home in Gonaives that night around 1 am. They found Kevs in the downstairs bedroom first, tied his hands behind his back with a strong cord, put a gun to his head and forced him to call out to us from the other side of our bedroom door to get us to unlock it.

We spent the next 2 hours in shock as these men pulled open drawers, emptied the contents on the floor, went through my jewelry box, our filing cabinets, held a knife to Beaver's throat while he opened the safe in our room. They tied Beaver up and made him lay on his side on the floor. They flipped the mattress I was on and then tied my hands together and left me more or less pinned to the far wall with the mattress as a buffer.

They never hurt us. I want to make that very clear. They threatened us. They kept demanding the guns and bags of money that they were certain we had hidden somewhere. They grabbed all our computers, I pads and phones within seconds of entering the room. We don't own any guns. There were no bags of money. This made them all the angrier. But they never hurt us.

And in a way it seemed, they too were scared.

There were times when I would start singing a popular song in Haiti at that time. "Bondye, n bezwen w kounye a" (Good God, we need you now). It was a song stuck in my head and in this precarious situation, it was also stuck on my lips. I was singing it out loud without even realizing it. At one point the tallest gentleman, the one holding the large knife, rushed to me, held the knife in front of my face, and demanded:

Sispan. Stop singing. Stop singing that song.

And that is when I realized how very scared he was. He was shaking. I came to know then that he was indeed a believer. His was not a faith, but rather a knowing that if I invoked this Good God to come into the room, He indeed would. So I said to him,

Listen brother, God is here and he knows you and loves you. It is a good thing that we invite him.

Yeah, he wasn't having it. But that encounter did boost my own faith. I can thank him for that.

They took Kevs from the room and told us if we moved they would kill us. But they took him to navigate the rest of the house and their escape. They figured as long as they had him as a hostage, we wouldn't come after them with the guns they assumed we still had.

Beaver got across the room to me and we spontaneously began singing in whispered voices choruses about the goodness of God. Which seems so far-fetched to me now as I write it. We sang. We called angels around our son. Every few minutes one of the men would come in and check to make sure we were still tied up while the others went through the house looking for anything of value.

During this whole episode I realized I had to choose between:

1. Staying in the present, with what was happening at the moment
2. Or thinking about all the ways the night could end and go insane.

Having control of my mind was my single most important weapon.

The sordid possibilities of how this could go were slamming into my brain. Would they shoot my husband in front of me? Would they try to kidnap my son? Would they go after my body? All the unthinkables were offering themselves to me in rapid succession.

Then the Voice of Heaven whispered to me,

Stop imagining the worst.
Pay attention to what actually IS.
Stay in the PRESENT.
This is how you will survive.

And that was entirely doable, and it was entirely my choice.

In everyday life, how much anxiety do we let in because we let our minds imagine the worst-case scenarios? This will eat us alive if we let it.

My advice: When you start to spiral with what ifs, stop, and look around. Remind yourself of the real things that surround you. Acknowledge what actually is. Say it out loud if you can.

Even with four armed men ransacking our room and holding us hostage, I had to use my power to acknowledge what was still good.

- No one has been hurt to this point.
- We were still all together.
- We were still breathing.
- My voice still worked. My fingers and toes, too.

Any good thing at all, I had to grab and acknowledge the truth.

I raised my kids to practice gratitude when days got rough. This is the same thing, on steroids.

During these moments of the invasion, I realized I could go ahead and pray for our kids in the USA that would hear about this event in the hours to come. Proactive acts at their best!

I prayed that God would pre-heal them from the trauma of the news they would hear in the early morning hours, however, this story came to an end.

I prayed for myself too. I prayed that God would go ahead and start healing me from the incident not yet over. My thought was, *ain't nobody got time for this.* I have stuff to do and a company to build and I can not take time to get sidelined from this nonsense. Please God, go ahead and start healing my brain.

Seriously.

So here I was three years later, in the office of an amazing woman who asked the right question that ripped open the pulsing wound and led me into the next steps of this process. I had already experienced massive amounts of healing. We were able to sleep in our bedroom that very next night. It never felt icky to me. And I never wanted to leave Haiti. I was never afraid of Haitian men after the event. I had no fear walking alone in the city or out riding my bike. There was a sweet healing of my frazzled emotions already underway.

But this bit required the professionals!

I was introduced to Eye Movement Desensitization and Reprocessing (EMDR) therapy and it worked! I don't fully understand how it works. I think it has to do with reconnecting with your body in the midst of traumatic memories. Kind of resetting your system: that you are in fact alive and you survived the event so that the trauma is not re-lived over and over again every time it gets triggered.

I'm not going to lie and say that I have no struggles with anxiety now. I used to feel ashamed for uncontrollable attacks. But not now. Now I know that anxiety is a chemical reaction to emotions being triggered in certain situations.

It is just information. Good information.

Your smart body is telling you something, my therapist explained. *How can that be shameful?*

So now when I feel something, I stop and say kindly, *Oh, body, look at you. What you got going on there? Thank you for letting me know we need to pay attention to this. You are doing a great job informing me! You're so smart!*

Then I usually ask that Voice to get to the bottom of it. Because generally the roots are buried deep.

And yes, it does take talking to my body as I would a good friend. She is. Honestly, she has been with me from the very beginning. Never leaving me no matter how horrible I treat her. I work her to the bone, think unkind things about her at times, shame her for aging and all the while she houses this person and takes me wherever I want to go. She has carried my kids from conception onward. She interprets the world for my brain to understand. She moves to the music in such a way that makes my whole sense of self be at peace. Yes, I am learning to talk kindly to her and love her as the dearest of friends.

The unfortunate truth is that traumatic events happen everywhere. They take place in our hometowns, in our kitchens, at school, and at the local movie theater. They can occur in all places we expect to be safe. It's no more or less traumatic because it happened to us in Haiti.

The important piece is to know that it changed me. It changed my brain. I thought I was ok, and I wasn't. And since I am painfully honest here, my hope is that I can be a part of the movement to normalize therapy. And that wherever and whenever traumas occurred others will recognize the need to get help.

~ 40 ~

ANGER, DEAR FRIEND.

"IF SOMEONE STRIKES YOU ON ONE CHEEK,
TURN TO HIM THE OTHER ALSO.
AND IF SOMEONE TAKES YOUR CLOAK,
DO NOT WITHHOLD YOUR TUNIC AS WELL."
LUKE 6:29

I was called back to these words of our radical rabbi.

I've struck my cheek on the pavement after being mugged on my bike and had more than a shirt taken from my home. And apparently, I have lost the grace to walk this out well. I am clearly not winning at losing.

I had this embarrassing incident, where I yelled accusingly at a man carrying a ladder off our property. A ladder the same make and color of a ladder that is ours. Except it wasn't ours, it was his.

He wasn't angry, he understood the mistake.

But I had no inclination whatsoever (if it was indeed our ladder) to also offer him a hammer or a power drill.

I have become reactionary and suspicious. I've let my heart get small and victim-y.

I've made too much space for Anger.

O Anger, faithful friend!

When people do bad things to us, and it hurts like hell, you come running!

Always. You show up quickly because you know what we feel. You just know.

You are our friend in battle. Your presence tells others to stay back. Most people are scared of your hot temper and strong words. People know to keep their distance when you are in the house.

And I think it's ok for you to come and sit on the porch awhile. You help us process what we have been through and feel all those twisty feelings.

But friend, you don't get to live here. I know that is always disappointing to you. So disappointing.

The truth is, if I let you stay, I'll have to move someone out to make space for you. You insist you won't take up much room. *I'll just sleep on the couch, don't worry,* you say to me so generously.

But we both know the truth. If you come in, you'll start leaving your socks in the bathroom and your dirty dishes in the sink. Your stuff ends up spread out in every room. And before we know it, Love, Humility, Vulnerability, Kindness and Generosity have all shrunk back. And some are even camping in the backyard because ultimately, you cannot coexist.

Before long I start yelling accusations at innocent people simply carrying their tools from the site.

So friend, Anger, thanks for showing up and wanting to protect me from ever getting hurt again by creating a hard shield of protection.

But in a few days, you're going to have to throw on your backpack and head out.

See, even though your company feels good when I am broken and my heart is smashed to pieces, you can't move in.

You cannot live here.

~ 41 ~

KINDNESS BROKE ME

"KINDNESS IS LOVE MADE VISIBLE."
H. SWANEPOEL, RAKTIVIST

I took a second bike ride late one afternoon and made it home just as the bottom fell out of the sky and the thunderstorm hit. I don't usually need two rides in a day, but that particular day ended in tears and hopping on my bike and pedaling is my best therapy.

The day before had been the difficult day. There were accusations and raised voices from misunderstandings and fear. I spent the day trying to patch things up and run interference.

But today it was Kindness that did me in.

Sometimes I feel like all my colleagues see in me is this ranting, uptight, lady boss. Because I see the desperate bank account that no one else sees. I know the bills that we must pay. I know the full effect of the innocent but costly mistake that was just made. In the stress of all this information, I am often not my best self.

It is intense to do business. Everywhere. Everyday. Haiti is no exception! Apparently USA is ranked #6 in the "Ease of Doing Business" index and Haiti is ranked #181. So there's that. An entire book could be written about what makes that so.

But on the "two bike ride" day, a couple of the young women in the sewing group did extra work for me personally and when I went to pay them for it, they said no, they would not accept it. They wanted to do it from their hearts. For me.

The kindness of their expressions did me in. These are people that are well aware of my weaknesses and stressful reactions. They see me every day. And still, such kindness! My eyes let loose the dam that had held the salty tears in place.

And I realized my tears were only confusing everyone.

Why is she crying when we are being nice? And why wasn't she crying yesterday when we had a very unhappy, very angry staff member roaming the building?

But no, it was the day of beauty and kindness that caused the tears and pushed me out the door for that second ride. It was the Kindness that broke me.

~ 42 ~

I HAVE A NEW TRICK.

" EVERY PROBLEM WE ENCOUNTER HAS A GIFT HIDDEN INSIDE IT."

UNKNOWN

I like gifts.

So I developed this new trick. I use my Super Power "Imagination" and I envision large problems as big hairy monsters coming toward me, scowling, slobbering, stinking and working hard to intimidate me with their messiness. But hidden in the hand that is unseeable behind their back, is an elaborate gift-wrapped box. And in the box is a really great present that I have been wanting.

And the only way to receive that gift is to turn toward the Big Hairy Scary Thing and face it head-on. Greet it like a friend. *Hi, so what have you got hiding here for me, you ugly stinking problem?*

I have two great examples of this. One is professional and would make you think I am pretty great probably. But who wants to read a story like that? Ha!

I'll tell you about this one instead. This one, painfully honest.

We used to be generous with our apartment/living space in Haiti. It has running water and even an air conditioner that works in the bedroom when the power is on. We have let others use it when we are out of town.

One time we were away for a long weekend and left the keys with a trusted friend who also lived in the city. To our shock and surprise, we came home to find our little apartment not at all as we left it. Dirty dishes piled up in the sink and food spilled on the counter. Clothes that apparently had been washed were now draped all over our living space for drying. Empty beverage bottles were scattered about.

At first, I could not believe what I was seeing.
What the what?

I thought I knew who had stayed over the weekend, but I never in my wildest imagination would have expected them to leave it like this. My emotions jumped back and forth from hurt to rage.

Now, to avoid conflict, my normal scaredy-cat self wanted to start folding clothes and washing dishes. Clean it up and never mention how we found it.

But then I remembered my new trick. And I remembered how dear this person was to me.

So there was no choice but to face the big hairy monster that was standing in front of me in the form of a very awkward, and painful conversation. Believing there was a gift hiding in there.

See, the truth is that I was angry. And that anger was going to find a way out one way or another. And honestly, I placed so much value on the relationship, I decided I'd rather risk hurting it with honesty, than with backhanded resentment.

So I pulled up my big girl pants and did just that. And, it was awful. It was awful describing the mess. It was awful questioning my friend's behavior. It was awful admitting how it hurt.

For a fraction of a moment, the person began to justify the situation. Then they stopped, looked me in the face, and said, *No, I'm not going to do that. I am going to say I am sorry. That was disrespectful and I am embarrassed. We did not handle that gift of your space well. I am sorry. We will fix it.*

And there it was. This person will tell you today that they never felt more safe and more love from me than they did that day that I came to them in an honest confrontation. We took a huge step TOWARD each other in that horrible awkward moment. And I hated walking myself to them. I hated calling them out. Hated it. It was indeed a big scary monster, BUT, it indeed carried a gift. To this day this friendship remains intact.

So, on the professional note, I once received an email from a client, a big client that makes large quantity orders with us. It was the kind of email you never want to open. We had made a mistake on a 1000 piece order. 1000 pairs of earrings were not constructed well and they were writing to tell us they would be sending them back. Of course, there was no money to refund them, it was long ago spent on materials and labor. It was a lot of money we didn't have and a lot of humiliation because we had not delivered the product they had paid for.

And then I remembered. This is a humongous, scary, monster-looking thing and in its left hand hiding behind its back is a tiny gift-wrapped box of something I have been wanting.

So I turned toward the email and reread it. I still felt sick to my stomach as I did. This is what I wrote:

Thank you.

We are of course mortified. Rightly so.

You are right in that we don't want pity purchases any more than you do.
And that we aren't doing each other a favor if we aren't honest about problems.
We hear your heart in the email and we thank you.

Please ship them back to us. We will salvage what we can. But we are sorry to say that we are not confident we can remake these pieces to spec.
The wood pieces are not made in-house and the gentleman in Port that made them was pressed to get them made as is. I am very sorry to say this.

We'd like to offer you these other options.
These are three of my personal favorites and they are also three that I have confidence in creating 1000 pairs in the same quality in a timely manner.

You guys are the best company to work with. We feel very aligned with you in terms of mission and vision and heart. I know this was an awful email to have to write, as much as it was awful to receive a product not up to the standards you expect.

Again, we are deeply sorry for the problems this creates for you. We never want to be that company!

Please let us know if any of these three earrings will work. We can of-course send you samples of any that you'd like to look at more closely.

Grace upon grace,

****

I faced it head-on and responded. This is the reply I received from the company:

****

Hi Kathy,

I read your email to some staff members and they cried. We know how challenging this is on every angle and we truly appreciate your gracious reply.

****

All of that to say, I am learning to look at the things that make me squirm and even make me sick to my stomach, and turn toward them. There is a gift inside. Truly there is.

~ 43 ~

FAITH STRIPPED TO THE CORE

"PERFECTION IS ACHIEVED, NOT WHEN THERE IS NO MORE TO ADD,
BUT WHEN THERE IS NOTHING LEFT TO TAKE AWAY"
ANTOINE DE SAINT

Mine is a faith stripped to its core. Or pretty close.

I entered Haiti with a fairly plump collection of beliefs. The kind that has a nice neat Statement of Faith attached. All the boxes were checked so that I imagined myself in pretty good standing with any religious corporate body. So I was comfortable and confident carrying the party line tucked safely into my backpack as I waded across the ocean into my new world, Haiti.

All of these carefully curated items of faith remind me of the movie, *The Aeronauts*. The movie is about two people on a spectacularly dangerous flight in a hot air balloon attempting to reach an altitude higher than anyone had gone before. The basket that carries them and their many belongings is nicely furnished with the essentials for the trip; temperature gages, measuring sticks, binoculars, notebooks, drawing utensils, bandages and brandy.

Mid Flight, a huge storm overtakes them unexpectedly and the hot air balloon begins plummeting to earth. Frantically they begin shedding all excess weight. Things that seemed essential when they started the journey, are tossed overboard without a second thought in the face of losing their lives as the solid earth rushes up to meet them.

Life has a way of doing this for all of us if we live long enough. We can accumulate lofty belief systems and fluffy well-patterned statements of faith. But we eventually go through unexpected plummets, hit by gale force winds we never imagined. And what once seemed essential, solid and non-negotiable is seen from a very different perspective. We find that we quickly discard the decorative to grasp firmly to what is real.

My faith is like that.

Like so many other hot air balloon travelers, set out to do great things, my faith has gone through fire. The outer layers burned to dust. What is left is the real.

I am always safe in God's hands.
A counselor, with the greatest of intentions, asked me to repeat the declaration:
I could not.

It seems my mouth won't form words I don't know to be certain. My body is in this with me, and it just won't do some things. Like form words that might prove to be false in important moments. And Life has gotten far too precious for that. I can only say what I really believe to be true, wrapped as it is in the wonder of mystery.

What I can say is this:
Whether I am safe or not, God never leaves me. He/She/They stay.

They hold me and whisper in my ear their kind words through it all.

This I know to be true.

I can agree we are sent out to heal the sick and raise the dead. And sometimes, glorious times, I've seen sickness go quicker than meds would likely have done it. And I've heard hundreds of stories of people who have experienced those miracles.

And sometimes, I have tried with all the faith to do this and yet, people I love have died and babies stayed sick and we drove the vehicle to the hospital to receive the grief stricken mama and the baby's still body.

Whether we are safe or not, God never leaves us.
This I know to be true. My faith is trim and it is still faith.

Being Saved
In some circles of Christianity we are taught that the job of the converted is to go out and get people saved from the fiery hell that is awaiting in the next life, if they don't choose our loving God in this one.

I've become much more intimately acquainted with suffering. There is a cognitive dissonance I cannot overcome with imagining the God I know, to be the one hurling human beings into more suffering.

Perhaps I am wrong, but somewhere along the way, I shifted. My focus became Jesus' prayer found in Matthew 6.

Thy kingdom come
Thy will be done
On earth as it is in heaven.

This decree has become my center.

As I imagine it, Heaven has great art! Heaven has justice! In that realm our eyes are open to see the beauty in the ones to our left and to our right. In heaven there are not many people trying to lose weight while the others are starving for more calories. This notion of "On earth as it is in heaven" has become the North Star of my life and my faith.

You could say this was the thing that was NOT thrown from the basket of the plummeting hot air balloon!

It holds even now.

Holy Spirit

The Holy Spirit also graciously agreed to stay with me. This is a great relief. Even without the neat repeatable statement of faith. He has become my closest comrade. He doesn't mind when I go quiet for a while. He knows me. He answers my many questions and teaches me all the things, even when I call him bossy or smarty pants.

God the Parent

Father God has been joined with his feminine side. I am still quite new to this, but when I see a glimpse of God as Mother God, I am undone. To imagine that Father God is also equally Mother God and that She loves like I love?

Like I love my kids?

This is my body ripped open for you. Here, my milk, drink it, use my calories to provide for your needs.

I still need a lot of practice interchanging He and She. I'm working on it.

Jesus, the Christ

Jesus? Well, he remains the most courageous, spontaneous, mischievous and exciting big brother a girl could ever want. He is the one you want to come to all of your camp fires, because where he is there is good wine and good conversation and probably some wild dancing. He runs toward the sound of gunshots, not away. He picks up the woman covered in scabs from her death bed to hold her close and give her kisses one more time. Yeah, I am still a goner for him. Will always be.

If I take a breath or two, I can find Him. Sometimes he shows up in the knowing strong arms of my sister and in the tears of my brother. He shows up in the dread headed kid with his moonshine and dark glasses. He shows up in the robber and in the robbed. He always shows up.

Whether I am safe or not, God never leaves me.

No us and Them

Perhaps the greatest gift Haiti has given me as a recovering helper is the understanding that in reality there is no such thing as:

The helpers and the helped.
The haves and have nots.
The healers and the healed.

These are simply lazy ways to frame the world, so we can get on about our business.

There simply is no US and THEM.

We must get eye level with one another. We may come to the table from different directions, but we are all at the same table. Equal. All fully human. All eligible to learn. Having different life experiences? Yes, but our human experience is much the same.

When I've tried to share these ideas with others, I've had leaders of organizations ask me, *How do we change? How do we run our programs differently?*

I can't tell you that. I can only tell you that when our eyes see through the lens of respect and are able to find the beauty in the person across the table, it is felt by all.

When we come to the table in humility, acquainted with the grace that sustains us, it will be a different conversation. The program will run differently because we are different.

We tend to come into an area imagining that the story starts when we show up. We forget that this film started long ago. There are many actors at play, many forces for both good and not so good at work. I once heard a colleague speak about all the amazing things God was doing in a neighborhood, referencing the list of helpers running projects there. I was speechless.

What about the local people and the quiet signs of God at work done by neighbors who make certain the elder next door is getting food each day? What about the way older men teach the younger ones to walk with honor and integrity. What about the times children choose to carry water together, just because they want to help lighten the load of a younger one? What about the beauty in all of that? It was disturbing to think that people didn't see that part first. Before the helper's part.

Saviorism, the achilles heel of every Helper, is a tricky bit.

Is it wrong to want to share your food with fellow humans that are hungry?

Is it wrong to want to create jobs for the unemployed or schools where there are none?

Does that reveal your savior mentality? Or simply your humanity?

I've seen both and been both.

One says I am different than you so I will help you.
The other says I am the same as you so I will share what I have.

2ND STORY GOODS
we make stuff you feel good about buying

2nd Story Goods is part of MUCH INC,
A registered non-profit.
visit us at:

www.2ndStorygoods.com
(you can shop for some really great stuff here too!)

Learn more and find a place to donate at
www.muchministries.org

Kathy Brooks is an artist, writer, social entrepreneur and ally in the movement for justice. Originally from Atlanta, Georgia she spent a good portion of her life working with people in the margins of society in the US, Canada, and the Caribbean. Her writing is filled with painfully honest stories that will make you laugh and maybe weep a little!

She loves to ride her bike, hang out with her people, write and make stuff.